THE NATIONALIST MOVEMENT

YOU HAVE INTRODUCED WESTERN EDUCATION, WITH FREE-
DOM OF SPEECH AND FREEDOM OF WRITING. BUT SIDE BY
SIDE WITH THESE THERE HAVE BEEN GREAT EVILS.

G. K. Gokhale

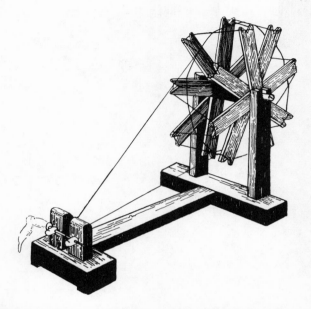

The Nationalist Movement

Indian Political Thought from Ranade to Bhave. By D. Mackenzie Brown

UNIVERSITY OF CALIFORNIA PRESS
BERKELEY AND LOS ANGELES

1970

TO PEG

University of California Press · Berkeley and Los Angeles
University of California Press, Ltd. · London, England
© 1961 by
The Regents of the University of California
STANDARD BOOK NUMBER 520-00183-4
Library of Congress Catalog Card Number: 61-11877
Printed in the United States of America
Third Printing, 1970

Preface

IN AN EARLIER ANALYSIS of the Indian political tradition published under the title *The White Umbrella
—Indian Political Thought from Manu to Gandhi,*
I dealt in large part with the early periods and philo-
sophic roots of India. This sequel is concerned with
recent and contemporary events. But the two differ
in more than chronology, though there is some over-
lapping in the periods covered. More important, *The
White Umbrella* was an interpretation of Hindu
theory as it developed in Indian history, whereas *The
Nationalist Movement* is an account of how that
theory helped to meet the crises of modern India—
crises that were precipitated by the inroads of Western
culture and by the struggle for independence.

While I have again chosen to build around a frame-
work of the life and thought of leading Indian personalities, there is this difference: Manu, Vyasa,
Vivekananda, Ghose were primarily theorists; Gokhale, Tilak, Lajpat Rai, Nehru are primarily statesmen or men of political action, although their writings are often profound. The decision to include
certain figures and to omit others is always a matter
for debate; this is especially true in choosing representative men from the latter group. Nonetheless, I
am confident that the figures selected for treatment
in this book are indeed central to the Nationalist
movement in India and embody its chief aspects.

The bibliography is limited to English-language

v

works cited in the text, commentaries, and notes. Detailed citations have been given with each chapter to suggest sources of additional material. These are not always of even quality, since some are given merely as examples of a particular viewpoint.

I wish to express sincere appreciation to those in India and America who have rendered services in the gathering and interpretation of material for this book. Acknowledgment is hereby made to various individuals and publishers for permission to use certain copyright material: Ganesh and Company, Madras, India, for excerpts from *The Indian Nation Builders,* by Mahadev Govind Ranade and others, and for quoted material taken from *Bal Gangadhar Tilak— His Writings and Speeches;* G. A. Natesan and Company, Madras, India, for portions of the *Speeches of Gopal Krishna Gokhale;* B. W. Huebsch and the Viking Press, Inc., New York, for passages from *The Political Future of India,* by Lajpat Rai; The Navajivan Trust, Ahmedabad, India, for excerpts from *Gandhi's Autobiography—the Story of My Experiments with Truth* and *Bhoodan Yajna,* by Vinoba Bhave; the John Day Company, New York, for passages from *Toward Freedom—the Autobiography of Jawaharlal Nehru;* Dr. Sarvepalli Radhakrishnan and the International Book Service, Poona, India, for material quoted from *Education, Politics and War,* by S. Radhakrishnan; and Sarvodaya Prachuralaya, Tanjore, India, for excerpts from *A Picture of Sarvodaya Social Order,* by Jaiprakash Narain.

I am indebted to the Government of India Information Services and to Consul Z. L. Kaul for the photographs used for the portraits of Indian leaders. My wife, Peggy Cheever Brown, did the title page spinning wheel sketch from material loaned by Professor J. M. Mahar of the Department of Anthropology, University of Arizona.

A research grant from the Social Science Research Council has aided in the gathering of material for this book.

D. M. B.

University of California
Santa Barbara
3 January 1961

Contents

Illustrations

The drawing on the title page was adapted from a common type of spinning wheel used in Indian villages. The wheel became a symbol of Gandhi's political program.

x

I

INDIA MEETS THE WEST

The inrush of a totally different civilization put an
end to all creative work for a time and an uncritical
admiration for all things Western took possession of
the mind of the educated classes, coupled with contempt for things of native origin. This was the first
time that the Indian mind was thrown off its balance.

D. S. SARMA

CONQUEST

In A.D. 647 the Indian king Harsha Vardhana
died without heir, leaving his empire in confusion.
Thus ended an age which, under the preceding Gupta
rulers, had seen the finest flowering of that magnificent
culture which had begun perhaps 3,000 years earlier
and developed a civilization firmly grounded in
universally accepted concepts of philosophy, religion,
and political thought. While the death of Harsha
was not in itself a major cause of the decline of
Indian culture, it marks conveniently a great

1

turning point of the country's political and cultural history. Not until our own day did the Aryan north regain a central control of its own destiny. Though south India experienced a later ascendancy, sporadic invasions of the northwest were followed by a tidal wave of Mohammedan conquest which placed most of the land under Moslem domination until the coming of European imperialism.

The arrival of European culture, particularly in its British phases, created a complex and unparalleled crisis in Indian culture and political institutions. The subjugation of the country by Moslems, centuries earlier, had shaken the structure of Hindu life. But great as that shock was it was not comparable in effect to the impact of European thought. The Moslems did not bring to India the humanism, the skepticism, the scientific thought and technology that were to be so devastating to traditional Indian life later on. Moslem economic institutions did not destroy village economy and native craftsmanship; Moslem political devices were understandable in terms of conventional Indian government, and they made full use of local political institutions. For democracy and socialism, those products of the European Renaissance and Reformation, had not at this earlier period revolutionized the body politic of India.

Paradoxically, the first impact of British culture served to revive and strengthen much of the classic tradition which had managed to survive through the centuries of decline after the death of Harsha.[1] The natural reaction to the collapse of Moslem domination was the revival of Hindu traditions, of

course, and this movement was strengthened by the
efforts of British Sanskrit scholars following the
pioneer work of Sir William Jones. Sir William had
published his translation of the Code of Manu, the
foundation of Hindu law, in 1794, and thereafter
British intellectuals became increasingly interested in
Indian culture.

Yet in the very revival of Hinduism there occurred
the seeds of doubt, inquiry, and reform which were to
bring about the crisis of Indian political thought
which forms the theme of the present study. That
crisis occurred and was intensified because, on the one
hand, the leaders and thinkers of the new India were
fired with a reverence for the great traditions of
Indian classic thought, and on the other hand they
were shaken by those elements in Hindu culture
which now, in the new light from the West, were to
seem degenerate, perverted, and reactionary. The
problem became more complex when it was realized
that this internal cultural struggle was at the same
time interlocked with the growing problem of British
economic and political domination. Add to this the
complexity of Mohammedan, Sikh, Christian, and
other religious minorities, with their sharp regional
divisions, each with its own distinct background, and
the result was an intellectual turmoil which defies
description.

Most foreigners, obviously, were not in any position
to assess the forces which they had helped to intro-
duce and release. The British attempted to remain
aloof from native life and to interfere only where
commercial or security interests were involved or

where such abominations as thuggee or suttee could not be tolerated, even under the loose system of established control. But they found increasing difficulty in reconciling imperial institutions with their own democratic ideals, until at last the firm sense of purpose inherited from men like Clive and Hastings, of a century before, slackened under the protests of a generation of English-educated Indian leaders.

WESTERNIZATION

Among the most characteristic aspects of Hindu life which survived the period of Mohammedan rule between the thirteenth and eighteenth centuries were the caste system, the joint family, and the self-governing village. A tradition of political absolutism at the state level and a background of philosophical hostility to the values of material progress further contributed to an environment which was not always hospitable to Westernization. And this same tradition was itself subject to severe destruction or reform in the face of technological revolution.

The Hindu caste system provided for a division of labor in society between the scholar-priest, the warrior-ruler, the business man, and the common worker. In theory, at least, the intellectual and the administrator were not directly concerned with economic enterprise, though indirectly they did have vital roles, especially in public policy. Trade and production were the provinces of the Vaisya caste. But with the coming of factory and store and bank, caste duties were forgotten in the scramblings of Brahman, warrior, and merchant alike to obtain the fruits of

4

trade and industry. And the servile Sudra, whose assigned caste duty was labor for the benefit of the higher castes, found a new power in the demand for his services in mine and mill.

The joint family system provided for the community functioning of all the living generations of a given family line. Except in Malabar, the organization was patriarchal: father, son, and grandson, with wives and children and other relatives, often shared a common home or group of homes. The male head of this community enjoyed almost dictatorial powers, though custom defined his rights and duties. Most important, the land and other immovable property remained with the male members of the joint family and was not generally distributed to female heirs. In an industrial era, this last feature tended to create great family trusts and family domination of certain industries. In the end, a Hindu Code Bill was to break down much of the legal support for the old joint family and open up its resources to the claims of its women and children.[2] But along with new opportunities would come new problems. The traditional family system provided a complete structure of "social security" covering old age, sickness, and death. Public institutions would in time have to be created to make up the loss, a loss that many Indians would feel could not be made good outside the family.

The self-governing village was a basic institution, in a nation composed of 550,000 villages. Whatever changes had been wrought in the past by war, invasion, and religious conflict, the village itself continued as an important political reality to the rural masses. Governed by a Panchayat, or committee of elders, it nourished and regulated Hindu life. Although British administrative control had weakened or destroyed the vitality of the system, the framers of the 1950 constitution of India were later to be so impressed with the value of the Panchayat that they would write into the constitution provisions for the perpetuation of the traditional village structure.[3] Meanwhile, the development of large-scale industrial enterprise would nearly destroy the basis of village self-government by destroying village industry. Dependence upon distant economies means dependence upon distant political forces.

The tradition of absolutism at the highest governmental levels was a product of the caste system, whereby political rule was the prerogative of a single caste, the Kshatriya or warrior group. Such a doctrine becomes untenable in an industrial age, when the Vaisya industrialist and the Sudra laborer hold the bulk of power. As in Europe, the development of democratic theories and institutions accompanied the rise of industrial enterprise. Yet if absolutism should return to India (and there are those who fear that it will) it will not be restored as a function of the Kshatriya caste. It will return under the impetus of a new theory of control.

India's background of philosophical hostility to the values of material progress is a result of the Hindu view of life. This is not to say that material welfare had no place in that scheme; but in comparison with ultimate ethical goals it had a subordinate place.

6

The "higher standard of living" which Americans accept, often as an unquestioned justification for various public policies, was not always to be considered a good in itself. For the Hindu, the Brahman especially, poverty carried its own virtues. Even for the lowest it was at least explainable: it was the inevitable result of the individual's behavior in past incarnations, and it served to purge and prepare him for better circumstances in his future lives. This did not mean that the more fortunate should not assist others, nor did it mean that rulers and officials should not do whatever was appropriate to improve economic and social conditions. But changes such as industrialization that destroyed the family and village structures were not to be considered "appropriate." Even if little improvement in conditions resulted, the existence of low living standards was not such a direct challenge to the accepted ideologies as it is today in an age of "democracy."

If Westernization challenged and disrupted the traditional culture patterns of India, these same traditions gave vitality to a counterchallenge to industrialism itself. It was accused of bringing greater evil than good, of creating soulless factories, slums, crime, and delinquent youth, of destroying village arts and crafts, and of causing mass unemployment and degradation.[4]

A major phase of this reaction was the movement for Swadeshi, or the boycott of foreign goods, in favor of Indian products. Gandhi himself led the movement against foreign goods and industries in favor of the so-called "cottage industry" and the "spinning wheel." A mill owner in India once wrote a plea to Gandhi to

INDIA MEETS THE WEST

stop his campaign for cottage production of cloth, on the ground that it was certain to bring ruin to the middle class mill owner. Gandhi replied characteristically, "This is a pathetic letter. I wish the correspondent's fears were realized. Then he would discover that the impending ruin of mills and shareholders of mills would be the time of their own and India's salvation. He would discover then that India would be pulsating with a new life and the middle class would be drawing their sustenance not, as now, from a starving peasantry but from prosperous farmers who would gladly exchange their produce for things they need but cannot themselves manufacture."[5] On another occasion Gandhi remarked, "The Noncooperation movement, with its intense belief in the power of the inner self to achieve wonderful things, has instinctively turned away from those machine made articles which appear to eliminate human toil and labour, while in reality they only increase them. There is one thing that may be truly said about the Khaddar [homespun] enterprise, in addition to its economic value—it brings us back to simplicity and self-reliance. 'If a man,' says the Chinese sage, 'has a machine-like heart in his breast, he has lost his grasp of pure unity, and becomes involved in complexity.' The complexity, in which Europe had become involved, undoubtedly led to the Great War." [6]

RESURGENT JAPAN

In their cultural turmoil, Indians had continually before them the spectacle of a resurgent Japan. They did not fail to note the example. When Tilak, the

8

Maratha Nationalist, organized the Ganapati festival in Poona to revive Hindu pride in Hindu life, songs were sung in praise of Japan and Japanese industrial achievement.[7] Tilak's newspaper, *Kesari,* in an editorial supporting Swadeshi, advocated giving preference to the purchase of Japanese manufactures above all except native Indian goods.[8] On another occasion the paper warned "A knowledge of the history and the rise of Japan has kindled in the people's minds a strong desire for Swaraj [independence], and if there is no gradual fruition of that desire, some of them, at all events, will not hesitate to commit deeds of violence in a fit of exasperation and despair."[9] The poet Tagore commented, "Japan's example has given heart to the rest of Asia. We have seen that the life and the strength are there in us, only the dead crust has to be removed."[10] For Indians, the Japanese victory over Russia, in 1905, was symbolic of the New Asia.[11]

The Japanese example strengthened the resolve of those Indians who wished to preserve traditional values at the same time that they embraced the advantages of Western technology. Swami Vivekananda, the militant Bengali reformer, remarked after a visit to Japan, "In my opinion, if all our rich and educated men once go and see Japan, their eyes will be opened. There, in Japan, you find a fine assimilation of knowledge, and not its indigestion as we have here. They have taken everything from the Europeans, but they remain Japanese all the same, and have not turned European; while in our country, the terrible mania of becoming Westernized has seized upon us like a plague." [12] Vivekananda's tribute was in recognition of the apparently successful Japanese attempt to combine tradition and technology.

But the Indian version of the problem was not so solvable, if only because India was under British rule, not to mention the complications provided by the Moslems and other cultural variants. The reform movement had to encompass at once the issues of independence, traditionalism, industrialization, communalism, and democracy.

II
PATTERN OF CONFLICT

> The policy of divide and rule is the sheet-anchor of
> all imperial governments. British rule in India has
> been persistently following that policy.
>
> LAJPAT RAI

TRADITION AND REFORM

The traditional religion of the Hindus was a
dual system. On the one hand it offered a philosophy
of life with concepts and ideals which might appeal to
the keenest of minds. But in addition to this theoretical system there existed an elaborate institutional
complex of duties, privileges, ceremonies, and super-
stitions, which gave form and meaning to the everyday
life of the individual. Theoretical Hinduism managed
to hold its own against the pressures of Western
agnosticism and Christianity. But practical Hinduism
suffered serious disintegration in the face of Western
standards and values.

The practice of suttee provides another illustration of the problem. On his visit to India in the thirteenth century, Marco Polo wrote of funeral rites he had witnessed ". . . his [the deceased's] relations proceed with great triumph and rejoicing, to burn the body; and his wife, from motives of pious regard for her husband, throws herself upon the pile and is consumed with him. Women who display this resolution are much applauded by the community, as, on the other hand, those who shrink from it are despised and reviled." [1]

Suttee, or religious suicide, found sanction in the Hindu Shastras as a demonstration of a widow's devotion. And in view of the pitiable plight of many widows, it may even have been welcomed by the latter. But as the passage from Marco Polo suggests, in time it came to be subject to so much social pressure that much of its significance as a voluntary sacrifice was lost. In modern times it has been repugnant not only to Europeans but to most Hindus as well. The nineteenth century Bengali reformer, Raja Ram Mohan Roy, led the fight against it and was "the first to make it an Indian question among Indians and transform it into an issue of national importance." [2]

As with suttee, so with other practices. Roy had pioneered the movement to reform traditional Hinduism by organizing the Brahmo Samaj. This movement was a response to Western ideas in general and to Christianity in particular. While it upheld the dignity of Hindu religious ideals, it supported other religions, stressed monotheism, and condemned such practices as idol worship. In the social field, Roy was particularly concerned with improvement of the status of women and with the abolition of caste discrimination. Suttee legislation was part of his program for the former, along with women's education, marriage reform and civil rights. Such reforms were logical applications of democratic theory, infiltrating Indian thought as a result of contact with English culture. Eventually, in the hands of a Gandhi, they would become weapons in the campaign for a new India.

Despite the eventual success of Indian reforms, it must not be forgotten that each issue was bitterly fought by contending groups within Hinduism itself, these struggles adding further confusion to the welter of debate that rocked the Indian mind of the time.

Had it not been for the dynamic power of such nationalists as Tilak, Vivekananda, and Lajpat Rai, Indian leaders might possibly have rejected in shame much of their rich heritage. But the Nationalists, while sympathetic to reform, pointed scornfully to the weaknesses and smug arrogance of the West. By their compelling oratory they stirred Hindu enthusiasm for Indian tradition and convinced many of their countrymen that Western institutions should be taken on Indian terms.

NATIONALISM AND THE BRITISH

On November 17, 1891 the London *Times* carried the following announcement: "The appointment of Mr. George Curzon to be Under-Secretary of State for India in the place of Sir John Gorst completes the series of official changes necessitated by the deaths

of Mr. W. H. Smith and Mr. Raikes. It will be generally agreed that no better choice could have been
made for the vacant post. Mr. Curzon's career at
Oxford showed that he possessed high natural abilities. And, what is perhaps more rare in the eldest son
of a peer, the steady industry which is required to
turn the gifts of nature to account." [3] This endorse-
ment was a justifiable estimate of the man who, in
another eight years, was to become Viceroy and "an
administrator of the highest distinction, who did
more for the material advancement of India than any
Viceroy since Dalhousie." [4] Yet such was his personality and such were the times that he "won a corres-
ponding unpopularity, partly by some of the measures
which he introduced, but mainly by some tactless
utterances, which expressed all too clearly his scorn-
ful attitude towards Indian aspirations." [4]

The symbol of Curzon's unpopularity was his partition of the province of Bengal. This disturbing
decision the Viceroy made in 1905, ostensibly for
administrative reasons resulting from the difficulties
encountered in handling such a large territory. Indian
Nationalists, however, considered it a calculated move
to split the militant population of Bengal, which,
having been first to receive Western education, was in
the forefront of the drive for the mitigation of British
rule. Also, since east and west Bengal were respectively
Moslem and Hindu by population majority, the
partition was viewed as a diabolical scheme to pit one
religious community against the other. Despite the
later rescinding of the partition order, Indo-British
relations never quite recovered their earlier degree of

harmony, and the trend of public opinion moved irrevocably toward anti-British feeling and the demand for independence.

Prior to Curzon's ill-fated policy there had existed a genuine respect for English rule on the part of most Indian leaders. This respect had a solid foundation in the very real capacities of the governing group. As far back as 1806 that astute observer of the Indian scene, the French Abbé Dubois, had commented on the British: ". . . the protection they afford to the weak as well as to the strong, to the Brahmin as to the Pariah, to the Christian, to the Mohammedan, and to the Pagan: all these have contributed more to the consolidation of their power than even their victories and conquests . . . For it would be hard to find a body of public servants better capable of filling with zeal and distinction the offices, more or less important, that are entrusted to them." [5]

Surendra Nath Banerjea, who presided over the Indian congress in 1895 and 1902, was among those who had believed strongly in the permanency of British imperial power because of the benefits of English civilization, which he was convinced was "the noblest the world has ever seen, . . . a civilization fraught with unspeakable blessings to the people of India . . ." In 1892, he said "we are the citizens of a great and free Empire and we live under the protecting shadow of one of the noblest constitutions the world has ever seen. The rights of Englishmen are ours, their privileges are ours, their constitution is ours. But we are excluded from them." [6]

This last complaint contains the burden of Indian

resentment. The English had taught too well. The brilliant products of British-founded universities at Calcutta, Bombay, and Madras were demanding the rights of Englishmen.

HINDU AND MOSLEM

The origin of the chronic stress between Hindu and Moslem in India dates back at least a millennium, to the tenth century. But the coming of Islam was different in its effects from the effects of the advent of invaders of still earlier periods, whose numbers and cultures had been quickly assimilated and absorbed by Hindu society. For the new Moslem way of life was based upon distinctly different foundations, and in those days Mohammedans were not tolerant of other creeds. The invaders retained strong ties with their home territories and with Mohammedan peoples to the West.[7] And the savagery of the conquerors, especially in northern India, left scars and divisions that have not been entirely erased to this day.

Despite the basic conflict involved in the two cultures, however, there developed a certain appreciation and interplay between native Hinduism and invading Islamism. Large numbers of Indians embraced the Moslem creed. Some conversions, it is true, were forced. But there was much in the faith of the conquerors that could appeal to the conquered, especially to the lower castes and the outcasts of Hinduism. The great majority of present-day Indian Moslems are descendants of such converts, rather than of the invaders themselves.[8] Moslem rulers, moreover, were not slow to make use of Hindus and Hindu institutions in their administration. High officials were drawn from Hindu ranks as converts, but later, even as unconverted Hindus.[9]

In time, a cultural interchange and fusion resulted that was to leave indelible impressions on the fabric of Indian life. This was most evident in the realm of art, but it was also significant in such fields as language, literature, and philosophy. Urdu, adapting an alphabet from the Arabic and adding a profusion of Persian words to the Indian, became the medium of Indian administration, transcending the provincial tongues. The related Hindi, using the traditional Hindu Devanagari characters and a vocabulary retaining more of the Sanskrit base, is now the official language of the Republic of India. The late sixteenth century administration of the greatest of the Moslem rulers, Akbar, was characterized by a remarkable degree of religious tolerance and communal harmony. An examination of that brilliant landmark of Moslem literature, the *Ain-I-Akbari* of Akbar's famous minister, reveals the profound appreciation by the Moslems of the whole spectrum of Hinduism.[10]

A devotional revival bloomed in northern India and united many of the precepts of Islam with India's traditional thought. Popular emphasis on monotheism grew. The universal brotherhood of Moslems challenged the caste system. Saints like Kabir symbolized the new union. From Nanak came Sikhism to create a new and living religion out of elements of both contending faiths. Where new institutions did not arise, individuals moved freely across religious bound-

17

aries into less orthodox sects. A Mohammedan mystic of humble birth who visited Akbar's court rose to become the recognized spiritual head of an order which is today exclusively Hindu.[11]

After Akbar, the intolerance and fanaticism of his great grandson, the Mogul emperor Aurangzeb, re-kindled the flames of communal strife. The resulting political problems, and those created by the forcible subjection of greater areas of Indian territory, could not be solved by the rapidly deteriorating administrative system centered at Delhi. Despite the healing influences of Kabir and Akbar, the peculiarities of dress, food, codes and ideals distinguishing Hindu and Moslem Indian provided bases of friction and rancor that led to persistent feuding and sporadic disorder.[12]

Eventually, against the background of Aurangzeb's ambition and cruelty, there arose among the rugged Maratha peoples of West Central India a fiery leader who was to symbolize the rebirth of Hindu nationalism and play a major role in reducing to ruins the inflated Moslem imperial system in India. Born in 1627, the noble Shivaji, by the time of his death in 1680, had built a Maratha state of such vitality that it could challenge the British for the succession to the Sultan's throne at Delhi. Three centuries later another Maratha leader, the irrepressible Bal Gangadher Tilak, was to institute a cult of Shivaji worship that quickened the political consciousness of his countrymen to work for the preservation of Hindu tradition and autonomy against the British and, incidentally, against the Moslem element.[13]

VIOLENCE AND NONVIOLENCE

Addressing an assembly of Indian nationalists on the subject of British rule, at Calcutta on January 2, 1907, Lokamanya Tilak said, ". . . your future rests entirely in your own hands. If you mean to be free, you can be free; if you do not mean to be free, you will fall and be forever fallen. So many of you need not take arms; but if you have not the power of active resistance, have you not the power of self-denial and self-abstinence in such a way as not to assist this foreign Government to rule over you? This is boycott and this is what is meant when we say, boycott is a political weapon. We shall not give them assistance to collect revenue and keep peace. We shall not assist them in fighting beyond the frontiers or outside India with Indian blood and money. We shall not assist them in carrying on the administration of justice. We shall have our own courts and, when time comes, we shall not pay taxes. Can you do that by your united efforts? If you can, you are free from to-morrow." [14]

Whether Tilak was himself a believer in Nonviolence has often been debated. His British critics looked upon him as a terrorist and quoted from provocative editorials in his newspaper, the *Kesari*. But he denied the charge and gave support to Gandhi's passive resistance movement. A recent biography states, "He read human nature and believed that violence was the law. But that was just philosophy. No one was a gentler person than Bal Gangadhar Tilak." [15]

Violence, however, there was, especially in Bengal

19

and Bombay. Bombs were thrown, officials murdered, and groups pledged to the violent overthrow of the British were organized. But their leadership faltered and their example failed to convince either the masses or the intelligentsia.

Aurobindo Ghose, for instance, abandoned his Bengal terrorist associates and took refuge in French Pondichéry. There he remained a recluse to his death, regarded by his followers as a modern saint.

Gandhi, who had developed the technique of Satyagraha, or "truth force," during his years in South Africa, was to become the leader of the Nonviolence movement in India after World War I. Nonviolent principles are variously stated in the Hindu, Buddhist, and Jain scriptures and were readily available to those who sought a method of combating British exploitation. Such a method, it was believed, would at the same time be effective against superior military force, would appeal to the Indian masses, and would prove morally correct and socially enduring. The principle of Satyagraha is the use of "truth force" to obtain a desired condition, whether individual or social. In contrast, the use of physical force is a confession of Asat, or "untruth."

The essence of the Violence versus Nonviolence issue, as seen by Mohandas Gandhi, Vinoba Bhave, and other leaders is that no permanent change in social institutions can ever be made without first changing the character and attitude of the individuals concerned. Any change by force, without a "change of heart," merely substitutes one master or evil for another. Nonviolence is thus the only truly effective method of social change.

But this philosophy of reform did not mean lack of struggle. On February 27, 1930, on the eve of the anti-British campaign, Gandhi, having spoken of his advice against the demonstrations in 1922, announced that this time, on his arrest "there is to be no mute, passive non-violence, but non-violence of the activist type should be set in motion, so that not a single believer in non-violence as an article of faith for the purpose of achieving India's goal should find himself free or alive at the end of the effort, to submit any longer to the existing slavery." [16]

The use of Nonviolence as a political weapon obviously demanded great personal sacrifice. In opposing unjust laws Indians were advised to court mass arrest by deliberately violating regulations, such as those prohibiting public assembly, and Gandhi himself led the famous "Salt March" to the Arabian Sea for the purpose of gathering salt in defiance of the government salt monopoly. Even in the face of severe beatings, the Satyagrahi disciplined himself to offer no resistance. Thus the Gandhian method was based on the insistence that the proper means was self-suffering, rather than the inflicting of harm or inconvenience on the enemy. Although these latter by-products might inevitably occur, they were not to be sought as direct results, in the way that ordinary passive resistance was understood in the West. Suffering, in itself, was held to be the purifying and transforming element. Thus it was a potent force much like that of religious sacrifice.

Gandhi's and Bhave's concept of violence can never be understood unless it is kept clearly in mind that violence must be defined by motive. The analogy of the surgeon is sometimes useful in this connection, since his merciful purpose is often accomplished by apparent violence to the body. On the other hand, the evil wish or thought embodies violence, even though it never results in action. In brief, the philosophy of Nonviolent reform which dominated the Indian revolution was a complete system of thought; it cannot be appreciated if viewed merely as a technique of political reform. Seen in this perspective, it is clear that in its purer forms Nonviolence is, as Gandhi proclaimed, a method not for the weak but for the strong.

DEMOCRACY AND DICTATORSHIP

Modern India received the impact of British democracy as an aspect of the heritage of Western culture. Ideas of popular control worked as a leaven in Indian political thinking of the nineteenth and twentieth centuries, serving to reinforce demands for self-government.

Along with democratic theory arrived the powerful influence of socialism. This greatly altered Indian attitudes on such matters as industry, British imperialism, capitalism, and party struggle. To many, socialism seemed to provide the explanation of, even the solution for, foreign political and economic domination. But eventually the conflict between the elaborate apparatus of the centralized state and the respect for individual and community which is implied by liberal democracy provoked serious stress in the minds of reformers who had attempted to embrace both aspects of Western thought.

Jayaprakash Narayan, leader of the Congress Socialist Party, was formerly an avowed Marxist who was convinced that a communist industrial revolution was the only solution to India's social problems. But after experience in Indian politics, he wrote: "It has become patent to me that materialism of any sort robs man of the means to become truly human. In a material civilization man has no rational incentive to be good." [17] And elsewhere: "The question is, how will . . . society be established? That can be done through an economic reconstruction which will ensure the fruit of labour to the worker. And that is possible only when there is decentralization in the economic field, when the system of production is organized on the basis of village industries. . . ." [18]

One of the most significant figures in the early Indian communist movement was the militant Bengali intellectual, M. N. Roy. He was "perhaps the first link between the Communist International and nascent Indian communism which was throughout the greater part of the twenties still at the level of ideas. It was in 1920 that M. N. Roy made his first appearance in Russia. Arriving that year in Europe, he placed himself at the head of a small but extremely virile group of Indian exiles in Berlin. He overcame all opposition and succeeded in securing his own recognition by the Moscow leaders as the spokesman of India." [19]

Roy believed that "Marxism is the logical outcome

of the scientific mode of thought" [20] and that since "rationalism dissolved the religious mode of thought in other parts of the world, that process must take place in India as well." [21] With these views he became an acid critic of all things traditional in India. His penetrating critiques of Indian life are among the most effective works of iconoclasm in modern times. But he extended this attitude even to Marxism itself. "Marxism," he wrote, "is a rationalist approach to everything. It is the rejection of all faith, even in Marxism. If we are true Marxists, we must . . . submit every single sentence written, even by Marx himself, to a scrutiny in the light of . . . modern science." [22]

This attitude led him to a break with the Communist Party so sharp that before his death he stood out as one of its severest critics, while he was himself denounced by former associates. Commenting on the Indian situation, Roy wrote: "The Asian mentality, being still largely mediaeval, is authoritarian and is naturally attracted by the idea of dictatorship. Therefore communism can easily infiltrate the nationalist movement." [23]

In the case of democracy, some leaders have demanded that it be taken on Indian terms and not accepted uncritically, as in the West. Dr. Radhakrishnan has expressed his own reservations on the subject: "We welcomed democracy as a release from autocratic rule, but we are not satisfied with its working today. We are coming to realize that government is a technical art and only those skilled in it can be the rulers. Democracy in its actual working rarely permits a country to be governed by its ablest men." [24] And in an earlier comment he insisted, "Democracy is not the standardizing of everyone . . . While the system of caste is not a democracy in the pursuit of wealth or happiness, it is a democracy so far as the spiritual values are concerned, for it recognizes that every soul has in it something transcendent and incapable of gradations . . . and insists that every individual must be afforded the opportunity to manifest the unique in him." [25]

When this problem of democracy versus authoritarian socialism is tied to the problem of means, the tendency of modern Indian leadership is to stress Nonviolent democratic means over socialist ends. But the element of social concern in Marxist idealism has had continued appeal, and the attempt has never been abandoned to seek, in one form or another, the goals which socialism promised.[26]

III

THE CONGRESS

The Congress is the oldest political organization we
have in India. It claims to represent all Indian
interests and classes. It is a matter of the greatest
pleasure to me to state that it was first conceived in
an English brain.

M. K. GANDHI

Iᴛꜱ ʀɪꜱᴇ

The patterns of internal conflict in India had
many aspects, touching the lives and institutions of
each area and each stratum of the varied population.
Nowhere is this so well revealed as in the founding,
development, dissensions, and triumphs of the Congress Party, the one supreme vehicle of the Nationalist
movement which had for decades been gathering
strength in India. Here, in caucus room and at conference table and locked in floor debate, are to be
found the Maratha and South Indian traditionalist,
the Bengali reformer, the die-hard nationalist, and

the Anglophile, as well as Hindu and Moslem, pacifist and terrorist.

Although a symbol of Indian nationalism, the Congress was paradoxically the brain child of a Scotsman of the Indian civil service, Allan Octavian Hume, Marquis of Dufferin and Ava, who distinguished himself as Governor General of India.[1] After some two years of discussion and negotiation, the first session of the Congress was held in Bombay in December, 1885. With the active approval of the British Government,[2] representatives from all over India met to discuss Indian affairs and offer suggestions for the improvement and modification of administration policies and actions. In that first meeting were many of the future leaders of the Indian Nationalist movement, some of whom were to remain stanch admirers and supporters of British rule, others becoming its bitterest foes.

It is possible to pick out of this movement a line of development and a chain of personalities revealing a coherent body of thought and action, from the very beginnings of the struggle against European rule up to the present stage of independence. At the outset, certain generalizations can be made: in the sphere of action with which we are primarily concerned here the Congress was largely a movement of western India, centering about Poona, Bombay, and Gujerat and including, at times, the Punjab and United Provinces to the north. Bengal, in the east, had been the first area to respond to the challenge of Western ideas. Beginning with Ram Mohan Roy, Bengal had produced a significant body of cultural and political thought that has given us such names as Tagore, Aurobindo, and Vivekananda. But while it was productive in thought and active in political protest it did not, with some exceptions, provide the main stream of organization and negotiation which would finally produce the Indian National Congress, the vehicle of ultimate independence.[3] South India, another important area, produced such impressive leaders as Krishnaswamy and C. P. Ramaswami Aiyar. But while there have been few minds as brilliant as those of this southern section of India, that area was too firmly established as the last stronghold of classic culture to react strongly to the political movements of the day, say with the same initiative as that of Bombay. South India had been comparatively free from the disorders of the Moslem conquest. The Sepoy Mutiny of 1857–59 had seared northern India, rather than southern, for in the south relatively little disorder marked the course of British rule. The genius of the Tamil mind seemed more devoted to the preservation of Hindu culture and to the appreciation of the best features of Western civilization than to reform, renaissance, and revolt.

The chain of personalities which carried India through its modern ideological crisis can be simply outlined: The main line of succession begins with Dadabhai Naoroji and passes to Ranade and then to Gokhale, Gandhi, and Jinnah. From Gandhi the movement stems to Nehru and Bhave and an independent India; and from Jinnah it stems to Pakistan.[4]

Strangely, the first figure in this chain, "the grand

old man of India," Dadabhai Naoroji, was not a Hindu but a Parsee. As a member of the Persian community in India he was perhaps naturally more understanding of Western institutions than the Hindus, with their accumulated Eastern heritage, the Parsees being among the most progressive of all Indian groups. He appealed, however, to all communities in India, regardless of cultural background, for he was one of the original founders of the Indian National Congress and for 61 years was continuously active in the political and social life of India. When he died at the age of 92, in 1917, his patient, peaceful, but persevering agitation for Indian self-rule had borne fruit in the creation of no less than 30 social and political institutions in India and in England, created for the welfare and advancement of the people of India. And he had inspired a series of leaders of such consummate skill and patriotism as has seldom been equalled in world history.

At the same time that the British liberal, Gladstone, was starting his Irish campaign in Parliament, Naoroji began his campaign for India, "educating the British on their responsibilities in India and demonstrating to them by relentless statistics and remorseless logic how India was being bled under the prevailing system of administration." [5]

For four years before the founding of the Indian National Congress Naoroji had been preparing India politically. His classic study entitled *Poverty and Un-British Rule in India*[6] was the early basis for political analysis and debate in his day, and he was universally recognized as the leader of Nationalist India. He did not confine his efforts to the Indian scene but directed the campaign from England as well. Gandhi tells us that "during my visits to England from South Africa I found that he had for an office a garret perhaps 8 feet by 6 feet. There was hardly room in it for another chair. His desk, his chair and a file of papers filled the room. Despite his personal means he lived in comparative poverty." In 1891, Naoroji ran for Parliament as Liberal Party candidate from Finsbury and was elected by a narrow majority over his English opponent.[7]

When Naoroji died, the Congress had reached the end of a long developmental phase in which primary emphasis had been placed on reform and protest, and on demands for greater self-government. Beginning with the latter part of the First World War, however, the Congress was to become a great force for Indian independence, translating its ideas of Swaraj into action both coöperative and noncoöperative.

Despite defections and dissensions, the tributary streams of Nationalist revival and revolt channeled into the main current of the Congress movement. Much of Moslem leadership in the early Congress was lost with the formation, in 1906, of the All India Muslim League, under the Aga Khan. The bitter split between radical and moderate Congress factions, in 1907, leading to the formation in 1916 of the Indian Home Rule League, was nearly fatal. Historical momentum and the advent of Gandhi, however, kept the Congress in the forefront of Indian politics.

It was a letter from A. O. Hume to the graduates of
Calcutta University, March 1, 1883, that was credited
with inspiring the Congress movement. Hume had
struck a note of service that found echo later in the
ideals of many Congress leaders. He advised, "Let
there be no more complaining of Englishmen being
preferred to you in all important offices, for if you
lack that public spirit, that highest form of altruistic
devotion that leads men to subordinate private ease
to the public weal, that patriotism that has made
Englishmen what they are—then rightly are these
preferred to you, rightly and inevitably have they
become your rulers. And rulers and task-masters they
must continue, let the yoke gall your shoulders never
so sorely, until you realize and stand prepared to act
upon the eternal truth that self-sacrifice and unselfishness are the only unfailing guides to freedom and
happiness." [8] Thus, at the outset, the issue of personal
zeal and integrity, with British leadership as the
model, was placed before restless India as the solution
to political discontent. In the years to come, even in
the depths of disillusionment with English policy,
this element of the problem would never be lost sight
of. And in such organizations as the Servants of India
Society, self-sacrifice for national welfare became the
guiding principle. Hume believed that if "only fifty
men, good and true," could be found to establish a
national organization dedicated to public service,
India's march toward democratic government could
begin under favorable auspices.[9] He was thus in-

31

strumental in giving structure to a movement which had begun with Raja Ram Mohan Roy's efforts, in the early decades of the century, culminating in the prohibition of suttee and the adoption of Western education. But Roy's "Westernism" was countered by the Arya Samaj traditionalism of Dayananda Saraswati and by the activities of the Theosophical Society. The latter, especially under the leadership of that remarkable English woman, Mrs. Annie Besant, attempted to preserve and promote Hindu religious and social ideals. The resulting conflict between reform and national rediscovery plagued the Congress organization and at times nearly destroyed it as an effective political agent.

Hume had originally envisioned an organization of Indian political leaders who would meet annually to consider "social" rather than "political" matters, but Lord Dufferin, the viceroy, thought otherwise. He persuaded Hume, and through him the most influential Indian politicians, that the new "congress" should debate and advise on current political and administrative issues. The first Congress meeting was at Bombay, in 1885, and dealt with specific grievances: A royal commission was requested to investigate the over-all administration of India. Changes in the Indian civil service examination system were suggested. The annexation and incorporation of upper Burma were protested.[10]

In those early days, when Mahadev Govind Ranade was a power behind the movement, the emphasis was on British good will and on social reform. These, in fact, became the policy of his pupil, Gopal Krishna Gokhale, and the main theme of the Congress. "The times and conditions would not allow in the earlier years anything else than a reasoned appeal to the authorities for the redress of grievances and a moderate demand of new concessions and privileges. This frame of mind soon developed into an art. Forensic talent on the one hand and a richly imaginative and emotional eloquence on the other, were soon brought to bear on the task that lay before the Indian politicians. An irresistible statement of facts followed by irrefutable arguments to prove the justice of the popular cause are to be met with everywhere in the speeches supporting the Congress resolutions and the addresses delivered by Congress Presidents. The burden of these utterances was that the English people are essentially just and fair, and that if properly informed they would never deviate from truth and the right, that the problem was the Anglo-Indian and not the Englishmen, that what was wrong was the system and not the individual, that the Congress was essentially loyal to the British Throne and fell afoul only of the Indian bureaucracy, that the English Constitution was the bulwark of popular liberties everywhere and the English Parliament was the Mother of Democracy all over, that the British Constitution was the best of all constitutions, that the Congress was not a seditious body, that the Indian politicians were the natural interpreters of Government to people and of people to Government, that Indians must be admitted into public services in larger measure, should be educated and made fit for high positions, that Universities, the Local Bodies and the public services should form the training ground for India, that the legislatures should be thrown open to election and the right of interpellation and discussion of budgets should be conceded, that the Press and the Forest Laws should be relaxed, the Police should become friendly to the people, that the taxes should be moderate. . . ." [11]

Two factors prevented this mild outlook from going unchallenged. One was the personality and zeal of Lokamanya Tilak and the other was the precipitation of conflict with the British by a series of issues culminating in the partition of Bengal. These forces came to a head in the Congress session of 1907, at Surat. Neither the moderate ("reform") group, under Gokhale, nor the radical ("nationalist") element, under Tilak, would yield. The result was explosion. "On the 28th [of December] the Congress met again. When the Presidential procession was passing, a slip signed by Lokamanya Tilak was handed over to Mr. Malvi telling him that he wished 'to address the delegates on the proposal of the election of President after it is seconded. I wish to move an adjournment with a constructive proposal. Please announce me.' The proceedings started at the step at which they had been terminated on the previous day and Surendra Nath Banerjea completed his speech seconding the proposal for the election of Dr. Ghose. This petition slip was not attended to, in spite of a reminder, and Lokamanya Tilak proceeded to the platform to assert his right of addressing the delegates. The Chairman of the Reception Committee and Dr. Ghose both thought Dr. Ghose was duly elected, and would not permit him [Tilak] to address the House. Shouting and confusion naturally followed, which was intensified by the fact that a shoe was hurled from amongst the delegates which grazed Surendra Nath Banerjea and hit Sir Pherozeshah Mehta. Then a general melee ensued. Chairs were thrown and sticks were brandished and the Congress ended for the day. The Moderate leaders met and organized the Convention and fixed a constitution for the Congress which practically excluded the Nationalists." [12]

ITS ACHIEVEMENT

The split in the Congress, although it left the moderate reform group in control, destroyed much of the effectiveness of the organization. Even the energetic efforts of Mrs. Besant to bring the two groups together, during the next decade, were unfruitful, largely because of Gokhale's fear of the power of Tilak. But in the end she was able to effect the establishment of a rival movement which offered a means for the promotion of Nationalist demands— the India Home Rule League.[13] In this work she was actively supported by such able leaders as B. P. Wadia and C. P. Ramaswami Aiyar. In 1916,[14] six months before Mrs. Besant, Tilak had already organized a Home Rule League in Maharashtra.

Time resolved the stubborn schism. The death of Gokhale, in 1915, and of Tilak himself, in 1920; the shock of the Amritsar tragedy; and finally the advent of Gandhi, brought a new synthesis to the Congress. And in the new theme, Swaraj (independence) was the goal, nonviolent Noncoöperation the means.

By 1929, the Congress had adopted the formula of complete independence. Even the proffered constitution of 1935 could not swerve Indian leaders from the immediate total goal. By 1942, "Quit India" was the official stand of Congress, and civil disobedience continued during the height of the Second World War. With the advent of peace, the British government faced the inevitable, and Swaraj became a reality. Later, after the triumph of Swaraj, we see evidence in the work of Narayan and Bhave that the theme of reform, so dear to Ranade and Gokhale, has not been forgotten and remains as a continuing evidence of the Nationalist movement.

What will history's verdict on the Congress be? Whatever the final estimate of this now aging organization, that of an Indian historian of its pre-independence phase is of interest here. "It has given battle to Government in a manner which no civilized Government dare condemn. Nonviolence, in thought, word and deed, has been the key-note of that fight and Gandhi has been acknowledged the Chief Constable of India. Government may have affected to abominate his cult of Satyagraha, but who can condemn the hold of Truth and Nonviolence on the affections of the people? In an age when royal families have been annihilated and monarchies have been upset and democratic constitutions have given way, in an age, too when the bi-party or the tri-party system of old has disappeared from politics and the rise of opposition is subdued not by defeating the opponent at the polls but by annihilating the party literally, to speak of non-violence may sound a mockery. Our recent experiences have furnished a fit and timely warning to us that the victories won through bloodshed are only maintained through bloodshed and lost through more of it, and that, when once force has become installed as the arbiter between two nations, it tends to butt in between any two communities and, for the matter of that, between any two individuals on all possible occasions." [15]

The first four political leaders discussed in the present study, beginning with Ranade, are concerned primarily with the educative or protestant phase of the life of the Indian Congress. The last five names are identified with a later period of action and responsibility. Through both phases there runs a theme of reform and revolution stemming from roots in both Indian thought and Western ideals. This is not a simple theme; it is overlaid with the complex pattern of conflict inside Hinduism, with stresses involving Islam and the British, and with issues of Violence and Nonviolence, democracy, and dictatorship. In the beginning, directed against British domination, the revolution as it continued proved to be a unique approach to the varied social problems of post-independence India.

IV
MAHADEV GOVIND RANADE

If Dadabhai Naoroji was the greatest Indian patriot
of the nineteenth century, Ranade was India's greatest
thinker.

C. Y. CHINTAMANI

Introduction

AMONGST THE SUCCESSIVE LEADERS of the Nationalist movement Mahadev Govind Ranade (1842–
1901) stands out as the first Hindu and the immediate
inspiration of the great Gokhale. The grand old
Parsee professor, Dadabhai Naoroji, had fathered the
Nationalist cause in mid-century, and no doubt he was
the model for Ranade when the latter was a student in
Bombay. But only a Hindu could have penetrated so
deeply into Indian social life or influenced so profoundly the attitudes of Hindu intellectuals toward
their own religious and cultural heritage. Ranade
taught and inspired a whole generation of Indian

38

youths destined to play essential roles in politics and government.

Intellectually as well as culturally, Ranade was well equipped for his task. His examination record at Bombay was so remarkable that it is said to have been sent to the University of Edinburgh as a model for Scottish students. In spite of time-consuming responsibilities in the Indian judiciary, Justice Ranade was able to produce monuments of scholarship that still stand as essential materials for the student of Indian social history.[1] Among these are his *Essays in Indian Economics* and *Essays in Religious and Social Reform*.

Intellectually distinguished, Ranade's unique quality was a trait of character, rather than of mind. Despite all opposition, all apparent failures, he never lost his calm, patient optimism in dealing with the British. Indeed, he was convinced that the association of Britain and India was a fortunate one for both peoples, and he was certain that an increase in knowledge and understanding of the mutual problems of Indians and British would inevitably remove the worst sources of evil and friction. In large measure, Ranade's patience and tolerance remained impressed upon the Congress organization and the Nationalist movement until the final realization of independence.

The tendency of the Indian Congress to pursue the dual and sometimes incompatible objectives of reform and independence stemmed largely from Ranade's outlook. He was a leading figure in the Indian Social Conference, a reform organization associated with the Congress in its early years. Indirectly, therefore, he was the source of much of the friction which later developed between the Nationalist and Reform wings of Congress, though it was he himself who resolved or smoothed over many early disputes arising from this cause.[2]

The following speech by Ranade was delivered before the Indian Social Conference at Lucknow, in 1900. It illustrates the breadth of the man's knowledge of Indian history, his critical attitude toward Hindu tradition, his tolerance and appreciation of Mohammedans and of Moslem culture, and his sensitivity to the need for communal harmony and social reform.

The Key to Progress

BY MAHADEV GOVIND RANADE

Last year, I had occasion, at the inauguration of the Conference held at Madras, to speak on the subject of "Southern India a hundred years ago." Today I find myself far away in the North, surrounded on all sides by the traditions of a civilization older than the oldest known to history, the land of the Aryan race settled in India.

I propose this time to draw your attention to the turn which Aryan civilization has taken under the influences represented by the conquest of this part of the country by the Mohammedans, nearly a thousand years back. The one factor which separates Northern India from its Southern neighbors, is the predominant influence of this conquest by the Mohammedans which has left its mark permanently upon the country, by the actual conversion to the Mohammedan faith of one-fifth of the population, and by the imperceptible but permanent moulding of the rest of the people in the ways of thought and belief, the like of which is hard to find on the Malabar or Coromandel Coasts.[3]

I propose to draw my materials from the Mohammedan philosophers and travellers who visited India both before and after the Mohammedan conquest changed the face of the country. Owing to the absence of the historic instinct among our people, we have necessarily to depend upon the testimony of foreign historians. That testimony is, however, unexceptional because it was for the most part given before the Mohammedan domination had effected the separation which distinguishes the old India of the past from the modern India in which we are now living. This domination also separates the line which marks off Southern India, of which I spoke last year, from the North, in one of the most representative centres of which we are met here today.

At the outset we must have a correct understanding of what Northern India was before Mahmud of Ghazni made his numerous expeditions for the plunder of its far-famed cities and temples, at the commencement of the eleventh century. Fortunately for us, we have a witness to this period of our history in the writings of Alberuni, whose work on India was written shortly after the time that Mahmud crossed the Indus as a conqueror of infidels.[4] Alberuni was a native of Khorasan, his birth place being near Khiva.[5] Mahmud of Ghazni conquered Khorasan and Alberuni had thus to shift to Ghazni, which was then the seat of a flourishing empire, the rulers of which were great patrons of Mohammedan learning. Alberuni was in special favour with Masaud, the son of Mahmud, and he was thus enabled to travel throughout India, where he spent many years, having mastered the Sanskrit language. He was a philosopher by profession and temper and had a special liking for Indian Philosophy, which he studied with the same care and attention that he bestowed on Plato and Aristotle. His work on India consists of eighty chapters relating to Religion, Philosopny, Caste, Idolatry, Civil Polity, Literature, Science, Mathematics, Medicine, Geography, Astronomy, Cosmogony, Alchemy and Astrology.

He took great pains to give a full description of all that was known to the Hindus under these several heads, and being naturally not a bigoted Mohammedan his book shows that he wrote his whole work with a single desire to promote the cause of true learning. While Alberuni shows a great regard for the Hindu Philosophy, Astronomy and Medicine, he was not slow in finding out the weak points of the Indian character. In his chapters on Caste and Idolatry, in the condemnation he pronounces on the want of practical aptitudes in our people and in their devotion to superstitious observances, Alberuni did not spare his censures. He contrasted the democratic equality of the Mohammedan people with the innumerable divisions of the Indian races. He notices the helpless position of the women of India and the filthy customs and the habits of the people in those days. He gives praise to the few educated Brahmans whom he separates from the superstitious multitudes, whose fallen condition he deplores. Even among the Brahmans, he notices the verbosity of their writings and the word-splitting which passed for wisdom. He notices the greediness and tyranny of the Hindu princes who would not agree to join their efforts together for any common purpose, and the timidity and the submissiveness of the people who, in his expressive language, were scattered like atoms of dust in all directions, before the invading Moslems. The prevailing feeling among the Mohammedans of the time was that the Hindus were infidels and entitled to no mercy or consideration, and the only choice to be allowed to them was that of death or conversion. Alberuni did not share in these views, but these were the views of his Master Mahmud of Ghazni and of the hordes who were led by him on these expeditions.

Another traveller Ibenbatuta, a native of Tangiers, in North Africa, visited this country about a hundred years after Kutbuddin established the Afghan kingdom at Delhi.[6] Like him, he was taken into favour by the then Delhi Emperor, Mohammed Tughluk, under whom he acted for some time as Judge of Delhi. Ibenbatuta travelled more extensively than Alberuni.

43

He travelled from the extreme West of Africa to the extreme West of China, and went around the Coast from Malabar to Coromandel. He was, however, not a philosopher, neither a scholar. His journal of travels is interesting, but he did not observe the manners and customs of the people with the same mastery of details that Alberuni's work shows on every page. The only points which struck Ibenbatuta in the course of his travels through India were the rite of suttee of which he was a witness, and the practice of drowning men in the Ganges, both of which struck him as inhuman to the degree he could not account for. He also notices the self-mortification of the yogis and their juggleries, in describing which last he mentions the fact that in the presence of the Emperor he saw a yogi raise his body up in the air, and keep it there for some time.

Another visitor Abdur Razzak reached India about 1450 A.D. His travels lay chiefly in the Southern Peninsula, Calicut, Vijayanagar and Mangalore. The narratives of two other travellers, one a Russian and the other a Venetian, who both visited India in the fifteenth century, are published by the Hakluyt Society, which afford most interesting reading. The general impression left on the minds of these travellers was a respect for the Brahmans for their philosophy and attainments in astrology, but for the common people, the vast multitudes of men and women, their sense was one of disgust and disappointment. Abdur Razzak expressed this feeling in his own words in a reply to the invitation of the king of Vijayanagar. He said to the king:—"If I have once escaped from the desert of thy love and reached my country, I shall not set out on another voyage even in the company of a king."

In Southern India, these travellers found that both men and women, besides being black, were almost nude, and divided into innumerable castes and sects which worshipped their own idols. This abuse of idolatry and caste struck every traveller as the peculiar characteristic of the country, and gave them offence. The practice of self-immolation or suttee and of human sacrifices to idols by being crushed over by the temple car are also mentioned.

Finally, we have the testimony of the Emperor Babar who in his memoirs thus describes this country: —"Hindustan is a country which has few things to recommend. The people are not handsome. They have no idea of the charms of friendly society or of freely mixing together in familiar intercourse. They have no genius, no comprehension of mind, no politeness of manners, no kindness or fellow-feeling, no ingenuity or mechanical invention in planning and executing their handicraft work, no skill or knowledge in design or architecture. They have no good horses, no good flesh, no good grapes or musk melons, no good fruits, no cold water or ice, no good food or bread in their bazaars, no baths, no colleges, no candles not even a candle stick. They have no aqueducts or canals, no gardens and no palaces; in their buildings they study neither elegance nor climate nor appearance nor regularity. Their peasants and lower classes all go about naked tying on only a *langoṭī*.[7] The women, too, have only a *lang*." The only good

45

points which Babar could find in favour of Hindus
then were that it is a large country, and has abundance
of gold and silver, and there is also an abundance of
workmen of every profession and trade for any work
and employment.

Such was the picture presented to the Mohammedans when they entered India through the passes
in successive hordes for three or four centuries. A
great portion of the disgust and disappointment felt
by these Mohammedan invaders may be set down to
ignorance and the pride of race. At the same time it
is always of advantage to know exactly how India
appeared in its strong and weak points to intelligent
foreigners such as those we have mentioned above.

The question for consideration to us at the present
moment is, whether, in consequence of the predominance of the Mohammedans for five centuries which
intervened from the invasion of Mahmud to the
ascendency of Akbar, the people of India were benefited by the contact thus forcibly brought together
between the two races. There are those among us
who think that this predominance has led to the
decay and corruption of the Indian character and that
the whole story of the Mohammedan ascendency
should, for all practical purposes, be regarded as a
period of humiliation and sorrow. Such a view, however, appears to be unsupported by any correct
appreciation of the forces which work for the eleva-
tion or depression of nations. It cannot be easily
assumed that in God's Providence such vast multitudes as those who inhabit India were placed centuries together under influences and restraints of

alien domination, unless such influences and restraints were calculated to do lasting service in the building up of the strength and character of the people in directions in which the Indian races were most deficient. Of one thing we are certain that, after lasting over 500 years, the Mohammedan empire gave way and made room for the reëstablishment of the old native races in the Punjab and throughout Central Hindustan and Southern India on foundations of a much more solid character than those which yielded so easily before the assaults of early Mohammedan conquerors. The domination therefore had not the effect of so depressing the people that they were unable to raise their heads again in greater solidarity. If the Indian races had not benefited by the contact and example of men with stronger muscles and greater powers, they would have never been able to reassert themselves in the way in which history bears testimony they did.

Quite independently of this evidence of the broad change that took place in the early part of the eighteenth century when the Mogul Empire went to pieces, and its place was taken up not by foreign settlers but by revived native powers, we have more convincing grounds to show that in a hundred ways the India of the eighteenth century, so far as the native races were concerned, was a stronger and better constituted India than met the eyes of the foreign travellers from Asia and Europe who visited it between the period of the first five centuries from 1000 to 1500. In Akbar's time this process of regenerate India first assumed a decided character which could not be well mistaken. No student of Akbar's reign will fail to notice that for the first time the conception was then realized of a united India in which Hindus and Mohammedans, such of them as had become permanently established in the country, were to take part in the building of an edifice rooted in the hearts of both by common interest and common ambitions in place of the scorn and contempt with which the Mohammedan invaders had regarded the religion of the Hindus, their forms of worship, their manners and customs, and the Hindus looked down upon them as barbarous Mlechchhas,[8] whose touch was pollution; a better appreciation of the good points in the character of both came to be recognized as the basis of the union.

Akbar was the first to see and realise the true nobility of soul and the devotion and fidelity of the Hindu character, and satisfied himself that no union was possible as long as the old bigotry and fanaticism was allowed to guide the councils of the empire. He soon gathered about him the best men of his time, men like Faizi, Abdul Fazul and their father Muberak, the historians, Mirsa Abdul Rahim, Naizamuddin Ahmad, Badauni and others. These were set to work upon the translation of the Hindu epics and Shastras and books of Science and Philosophy. The pride of the Rajput races was conciliated by taking in marriage the princesses of Jaipur and Jodhpur and by conferring equal or superior commands on those princes. These latter had been hitherto treated as enemies. They were now welcomed as the props of the empire, and Maharaja Bagavandas, his great nephews, Mansingh, for sometime Governor of Bengal and Kabul, Raja Thodar Mal and the Brahman companion of the emperor Raja Birbal, these were welcomed to court and trusted in the full consciousness that their interests were the same as those of the Moslem noblemen.

The emperor himself, guided by such counsel of his Hindu and Mohammedan nobles, became the real founder of the union between the two races and his policy for a hundred years guided and swayed the councils of the empire. A fusion of the two races was sought to be made firmer still, by the establishment of a religion of the *Din-I-ilahi* in which the best points both of the Mohammedan, Hindu and other faiths were sought to be incorporated.[9] Invidious taxation and privileges were done away with, and toleration of all faiths became the universal law of the empire. To conciliate his subjects, Akbar abjured the use of flesh except on four special occasions in the year, and he joined in the religious rites observed by his Hindu queens. In regard to the particular customs of the people, relating to points where natural humanity was shocked in a way to make union impossible, Akbar strove by wise encouragement and stern control, where necessary, to help the growth of better ideas. Suttee was virtually abolished by being placed under restraint which nobody could find fault with. Remarriage was encouraged, and marriage before puberty was prohibited. In these and a hundred other ways the fusion of the races and of their many faiths was sought to be accomplished with a success which was justified by the result for a hundred years.

49

This process of removing all causes of friction and establishing accord went on without interruption during the reigns of Akbar, Jehangir and Shahjahan. Shahjahan's eldest son, Dara Sheko, was himself an author of no mean repute. He translated the Upanishads, and wrote a work in which he sought to reconcile the Brahman religion with the Mohammedan faith. He died in 1659. This period of a hundred years may be regarded as the halcyon period of Indian history when the Hindu and Mohammedan races acted in full accord.

If, in place of Aurangzeb, Dara Sheko had succeeded to power as the eldest son of Shahjahan, the influences set on foot by the genius of Akbar would have gathered strength and possibly averted the collapse of the Mogul power for another century. This was, however, not to be so, and with Aurangzeb's ascent to the throne, a change of system commenced which gathered force during the long time that this emperor reigned. Even Aurangzeb had, however, to follow the traditions of his three predecessors. He could not dispense with Jai Singh or Jaswant Singh who were his principal military commanders. The revival of fanatic bigotry was kept in check by the presence of these great Rajput chiefs, one of whom, on the re-imposition of the Zezia, addressed to the emperor a protest, couched in unmistakable terms, that the God of Islam was also the God of the Hindus, and the subject of both races merited equal treatment. Aurangzeb unfortunately did not listen to this advice, and the result was, that the empire built by Akbar went to pieces even when Aurangzeb was alive. No one was more aware of his failure than Aurangzeb himself who, in his last moments, admitted that his whole life was a mistake.

The Marathas in the South, the Sikhs in the North, and the Rajput States helped in the dismemberment of the empire in the reigns of his immediate successors, with the result that nearly the whole of India was restored to its native Hindu sovereigns except Bengal, Oudh and the Deccan Hyderabad. It will be seen from this that so far from suffering from decay and corruption, the native races gathered strength by reason of the Mohammedan rule when it was directed by the wise counsel of those Mohammedan and Hindu statesmen who sought the weal of the country by a policy of toleration and equality. Since the time of Asoka, the element of strength, born of union, was wanting in the old Hindu dynasties which succumbed so easily to the Mohammedan invaders.

Besides this source of strength, there can be no doubt that in a hundred other ways the Mohammedan domination helped to refine the tastes and manners of the Hindus. The art of Government was better understood by the Mohammedan than by the old Hindu sovereigns. The arts were also singularly defective till the Mohammedans came. They brought in the use of gunpowder and artillery; in the words of Babar, they "taught ingenuity and mechanical invention in a number of handicraft arts," the very nomenclature of which being made up of non-Hindu words shows their foreign origin. They introduced candles, paper, glass and household furniture and saddlery. They improved the knowledge of the people in music,

instrumental and vocal, medicine and astronomy, and
their example was followed by the Hindus in the
perversions of both these sciences, astrology and alchemy, geography and history were first made possible
departments of knowledge and literature by their
example. They made roads, aqueducts, canals, caravan-
saries and the post office, and introduced the best
specimens of architecture, and improved our garden-
ing and made us acquainted with a taste of new
fruits and flowers. The revenue system, as inaugurated by Thodar Mal in Akbar's time, is the basis
of the revenue system up to the present day. They
carried on the entire commerce by sea with distant
regions, and made India feel that it was a portion of
the inhabited world with relations with all, and not
cut off from all social intercourse. In all these re-
spects, the civilization of the united Hindu and
Moslem powers represented by the Moguls at Delhi,
was a distinct advance beyond what was possible
before the tenth century of the Christian era.

More lasting benefits have, however, accrued by
this contact in the higher tone it has given to the
religion and thoughts of the people. In this respect
both the Mohammedans and Hindus benefitted by
contact with one another. As regards the Mohammedans, their own historians admit that the Sufi
heresy gathered strength from contact with the Hindu
teachers, and made many Mohammedans believe in
transmigration and in the final union of the soul with
supreme spirit. The Moharam festival and saint worship are the best evidence of the way in which the
Mohammedans were influenced by Hindu ideas. We

are more directly concerned with the way in which this contact has affected the Hindus. The prevailing tone of pantheism had established a toleration for polytheism among our most revered ancient teachers who rested content with separating the few from the many, and established no bridge between them. This separation of the old religion has prevented its higher precepts from becoming the common position of whole races. Under the purely Hindu system, the intellect may admit but the heart declines to allow a common platform to all people in the sight of God.

The Vaishnava movement, however, has succeeded in establishing the bridge noted above.[10] The purification of the Hindu mind was accomplished to an extent which very few at the present moment realize in all its significance. The Brahmo and the Arya Samaj movements of this century are the continuations of this ethical and spiritual growth. Caste, idolatry, polytheism and gross conceptions of purity and pollution were the precise points in which the Mohammedans and the Hindus were most opposed to one another, and all the sects named above had this general characteristic that they were opposed to these defects in the character of our people. The abuses of polytheism were checked by the devotion to one object of worship which in the case of many of these Vaishnava sects was supreme God, the Paramatma and the abuses of caste were controlled by conceding to all Hindus and Mohammedans alike the right to worship and love one god who was the god of all. In the case of the Sikhs the puritanic spirit even developed under persecution, into a coarse imitation of the Mohammedan fanaticism directed against the Mohammedans themselves, but in the case of the other sectaries, both old and new, the tolerant and suffering spirit of Vaishnavism has prevailed, breathing peace and good-will towards all.

Such are the chief features of the influences result-ing from the contact of Mohammedans and Hindus in Northern India. They brought about a fusion of thoughts and ideas which benefited both communities, making the Mohammedans less bigoted and the Hin-dus more puritanic and more single-minded in their devotion. There was nothing like this to be found in Southern India as described by Dubois where the Hindu sectarian spirit intensified caste, pride and idolatrous observances. The fusion would have been more complete but for the revival of fanaticism for which Aurangzeb must be held chiefly responsible. Owing to the circumstances, the work of fusion was left incomplete; and in the course of years, both the communities[11] have developed weaknesses of a charac-ter which still need the disciplining process to be continued for a longer time under other masters. Both Hindus and Mohammedans lack many of those virtues represented by the love of order and regulated authority. Both are wanting in the love of municipal freedom, in the exercise of virtues necessary for civic life and in aptitude for mechanical skill, in the love of science and research, in the love and daring and adventurous discovery, the resolution to master difficulties and in chivalrous respect for womankind. Neither the old Hindu nor the old Mohammedan civilization was in a condition to train these virtues

The Key to Progress

in a way to bring up the races of India on a level with those of Western Europe and so the work of education had to be renewed, and it has been now going on for the past century and more under the *Pax Britannica* with results which all of us are witnesses to in ourselves.

If the lessons of the past have any value, one thing is quite clear, that in this vast country no progress is possible unless both Hindus and Mohammedans join hands together and are determined to follow the lead of the men who flourished in Akbar's time and were his chief advisers and councillors and sedulously avoid the mistakes which were committed by his great-grandson Aurangzeb. Joint action from a sense of common interest and a common desire to bring about the fusion of the thoughts and feelings of men so as to tolerate small differences and bring about concord, these were the chief aims kept in view by Akbar and formed the principle of the new divine faith formulated in the *Din-I-ilahi*. Every effort on the part of either Hindus or Mohammedans to regard their interests as separated and distinct and every attempt made by the two communities to create separate schools and interests among themselves, and not to heal up the wounds inflicted by mutual hatred of caste and creed, must be deprecated on all hands. It is to be feared that this lesson has not been sufficiently kept in mind by the leaders of both communities in their struggle for existence and in the acquisition of power and predominance during recent years. There is at times a great danger of the work of Akbar being undone by losing sight of this great lesson which the history of his reign and that of his two successors is so well calculated to teach.

The conference which brings us together is especially intended for the propagation of this "Din" or "Dharma," and it is in connection with that message, chiefly, that I have ventured to speak to you, today, on this important subject. The ills that we are suffering from are most of them self-inflicted evils, the cure of which is to a large extent in our own hands. Looking at the series of measures which Akbar adopted in his time to cure these evils, one feels how correct was his vision when he and his advisers put their hands on those very defects in our national character which need to be remedied first before we venture on higher enterprises. Pursuit of high ideas, mutual sympathy and co-operation, perfect tolerance, a correct understanding of the diseases from which the body politic is suffering, and an earnest desire to apply suitable remedies —this is the work cut out for the present generation.

The awakening has commenced, as is witnessed, by the fact that we are met in this place from such distances for joint consultation and action. All that is needed is that we must put our hands to the plough and face the strife and the struggle. The success already achieved warrants the expectation that, if we persevere on right lines, the goal we have in view may be attained. That goal is not any particular advantage to be gained in power and wealth. It is represented by the efforts to attain it, the expansion and the evolution of the heart and the mind which all make us stronger and braver, purer and truer men. This is, at least, the lesson I draw from our more recent history of the past thousand years, and if those centuries have rolled away to no purpose over our heads, our cause is no doubt hopeless beyond cure. That is, however, not the faith in me; and I feel sure it is not the faith that moves you in the great struggle against our own weak selves than which nothing is more fatal to our individual and collective growth.

Both Hindus and Mohammedans have their work cut out in this struggle. In the backwardness of female education, in the disposition to overleap the bounds of their own religion, in matters of temperance, in their internal dissensions between castes and creeds, in the indulgence of impure speech, thought and action, on occasions when they are disposed to enjoy themselves in the abuses of many customs in regard to unequal and polygamous marriages, in their desire to be extravagant in their expenditure on such occasions, in the neglect of regulated charity, in the decay of public spirit, in insisting on the proper management of endowments in these and other matters, both communities are equal sinners, and there is thus much ground for improvement on common lines. Of course, the Hindus being by far the majority of the population, have other difficulties of their own to combat with, and they are trying in their gatherings of separate castes and communities, to remedy them each in their own way. But without cooperation and conjoined action of all communities, success is not possible, and it is on that account that the general conference is held in different places each year to rouse local interest, and help people in their separate efforts by a knowledge of what their friends similarly situated are doing in other parts. This is the reason of our meeting here, and I trust that this message I have attempted to deliver to you on this occasion will satisfy you that we cannot conceive a nobler work than the one for which we have met here today.

V
GOPAL KRISHNA GOKHALE

> Gokhale never abated his insistence upon these twin
> principles: that advance must be constitutional ad-
> vance, deserved through the spread of enlightenment
> and education; and that the British connection was
> essential to the well-being of India.
>
> J. S. HOYLAND

Introduction

RANADE'S WORK and his social philosophy
were continued after his death by another Maratha
Brahman who had been his disciple for twelve years,
Gopal Krishna Gokhale (1866–1915). True to the
Ranade tradition, Gokhale worked closely and, on the
whole, cordially, with the British government and
people. He played the often thankless role of inter-
preting the Indian people to the British and the
British administration to the Indians. He served on

the Indian Legislative Council for years and won the respect and friendship of Lord Curzon himself. But he was no Anglophile. He did not hesitate to collide head on with Curzon and others, whenever he felt that British policies were running counter to the best interests of India. He was far from a tool of the British; in fact, his public speeches and writings constitute a monument of criticism of English rule.

For all his success as a parliamentarian, Gokhale lacked the attributes of a popular leader. His natural arena was the council chamber, rather than the village square. His personality impressed by its quiet charm and thoughtfulness, rather than by any enthusiasm or quick inspiration. He had "the remarkable knack of saying the hardest things in the gentlest language." [1]

At the time of the Surat Congress split his popularity reached a low level. The Nationalist forces under Tilak remained convinced that Gokhale had been guilty of deceit in permitting the "railroading" of the convention in such a manner as to exclude them. Like Ranade, he had no wish to antagonize British administrators, as the extremists in the Congress were willing to do.[2] But Lord Minto, at the time, wrote of Gokhale that "as party manager he is a baby—he is always whining just like a second-rate Irishman, between Dan O'Connell and Parnell." [3]

It would be unfair, however, to depict Gokhale as weak, or as a ward politician. There was a quality of steel in the man that gave lasting strength to the Nationalist movement, and it is noteworthy that he imposed upon himself the severest of disciplines. He was even instrumental in founding the famous Servants of India Society to recruit young men as "political Sannyasins" dedicated to selfless service for the benefit of India.[4] Gokhale, who had renounced pursuit of all other goals, characterized the ideal of the Society as "devotion to motherland so profound and so passionate that its very thought thrills and its actual touch lifts one out of one's self." [5] And to this day the Society remains a force in Indian public life.

The two salient characteristics of Gokhale's politics were his emphasis upon reform before independence and his use of negotiation in place of force. A critic has commented that his methods and those of the Ranade school were correct for the reform programs, after independence, but not for Swaraj movements.[6] Nevertheless, his vigorous speaking campaigns in England and elsewhere undoubtedly did much to sow the seeds of criticism of British imperial policy among the British themselves. Even his Brahman rival, Tilak, with whom he had a bitter dispute, paid Gokhale deep homage at the time of his death, May 10, 1915: "This diamond of India, this jewel of Maharashtra, this prince of workers is taking eternal rest on the funeral ground. Look at him and try to emulate him . . . Like a triumphant hero he is passing away after having made his name immortal." [7]

The following speech was delivered in London, in 1905, before the New Reform Club. Especially interesting are his repeated references to Japanese progress, his expressed resentment against Curzon and partition, and his assertions of an underlying confidence in the reasonableness of Englishmen in general.

The Governing Caste

BY GOPAL KRISHNA GOKHALE

It was in 1833 that your Parliament announced to the people of India that the Government of the country would be so conducted that there would be no governing caste in that country, and that the rule would be one of equality for the two races in that land.[8] Three-fourths of a century have since elapsed, and still you not only find a governing caste in that land, but that caste is as vigorous, as dominant, as exclusive as ever.

It was, perhaps, inevitable that in the earlier years of your rule, when an administrative machinery of the Western type had to be introduced into India, all power should be placed in the hands of English officials, who alone then understood Western standards of government. But now that the schools and colleges and universities have been doing their work for half a century and more, and a large class of educated men have grown up—men qualified to take a part in the government of the country, and desirous of taking such a part—there is no excuse whatever for maintaining the monopoly. For the last twenty years the Indian people have been agitating for a greater voice in the affairs of their country, through the Indian National Congress. The bureaucracy, however, pays little attention to what we say in India, and so my countrymen thought it desirable that an appeal should now be addressed direct to the electors of this country.

The natural evils inseparable from a foreign bureaucracy monopolising all power have, during the last ten years, been intensified by the reactionary policy of the Indian Government, and this reaction and repression has been the darkest during the last three years. You have said, and I am glad you have said it, that my personal feeling towards Lord Curzon,[9] on whom the chief responsibility for the repression of the last three years mainly rests, is one of respect. That is so. I have been in his Council now for four years. And nobody could come in contact with him without being profoundly impressed by his great ability, his indefatigable energy, high sense of duty, and his devotion to the interests of England as he understands them. Lord Curzon is a brilliant and gifted man, and he has striven as hard as he could to promote, according to his lights, the interest of England in India. He has done several things for which he is entitled to great credit, but his main aim has been to strengthen the position of the Englishman in India, and weaken correspondingly the position of the Indian, so as to make it more and more difficult for the latter to urge his claim to that equality which has been promised him by the Parliament and the Sovereign, and which it is his legitimate ambition to attain. You will find—and I am anxious to be fair to Lord Curzon—that while he has done a great deal of good work in certain directions—giving larger grants to irrigation, to agricultural education, and to primary education, putting down assaults by Europeans on Indians, rousing local governments to greater energy, and so on—where he had to deal with the educated classes of the country and their legitimate position and aspirations, he has been reactionary, and even repressive. And it is this reaction and this repression that has driven my countrymen to a position bordering on despair.

Let me explain my meaning to you in a few words. There are four fields in which the educated classes, that is to say, those who have received a Western education—for we have our own Eastern learning, and men who receive that education are among the most learned in certain fields; but I am speaking now of Western education, because that education inspires one with an appreciation of free institutions—there are four fields in which the educated classes have been steadily making their influence felt, and in all those four fields the reactionary policy of recent years has sought to put them back. In the first place, a little local self-government was given us by Lord Ripon, and these educated classes naturally exercise much influence in that limited field.[10] Secondly, they are able to exercise some influence in the spread of higher education. Thirdly, they have a powerful Press, which in spite of defects inseparable from a state of transition, is steadily gaining in weight and importance, and its influence means the influence of educated Indians. Lastly, a few fairly high offices in the public service are held by Indians—almost everything worth having is monopolised by Englishmen—but a very few offices of some importance are allowed to be held by Indians, and appointments to these offices were hitherto made by means of an open competitive examination, with the result that men of ability who are usually also men of independence, had an opportunity of entering the public service.

Now in all these fields, Lord Curzon has put the clock back. Moreover, it is not only his measures, but also the manner in which he has forced them on the country about which my countrymen feel most bitter. I think this has been the result of the limitations imposed upon him by his temperament and his training. In Mr. Morley's "Life of Gladstone" one striking expression repeatedly occurs—it is what Mr. Gladstone calls "the profound principle of liberty." Mr. Gladstone says again and again that though Oxford had taught him many things, Oxford did not teach him an appreciation of the profound principle of liberty as a factor of human progress. Well, it seems other Oxford men, too, have not learnt how to appreciate that principle. Lord Curzon is no believer in free institutions, or in national aspirations. I believe if he were allowed a free hand he would hand the people of this country back to the rule of aristocracy that governed here before 1832. Well, Lord Curzon sees that the educated classes of India are pressing forward more and more to be associated with the government of their own country, and he thinks it is not to the interest of England, as he understands that interest, that this should be so. He therefore has tried to put back these men in every one of the four fields of which I have spoken. He has tried to fetter the Press by his Official Secrets Act. In regard to higher education, he has transferred the control of it to the hands of the officials and of such Indians as will always agree with the officials. Then, as regards the few fairly high offices open to us in our own country, he has abolished competition, and made everything dependent upon the pleasure of the officials, thereby enormously increasing official patronage, and making it more difficult for able and independent Indians to enter the public service of their own country. Lastly, he has tried to take away, especially in Bengal, a portion of that self-government which had been given to the people a quarter of a century ago.

As if all this retrogression were not sufficient, he ventured last year, in open Council, to explain away the Queen's Proclamation.[11] Ladies and gentlemen, it is with difficulty that I can speak with due restraint of his offending on this. The Queen's Proclamation has hitherto been regarded, both for its contents and the circumstances connected with the issuing of it, with feelings of gratitude and satisfaction by the people of India. It was issued on the morrow of the dark Mutiny by a Royal woman, in the name of a mighty nation, to a people who had just suffered most dreadful calamities in their own country. And I think England may well be proud of it for all time. The Proclamation assures the people of India that the Queen considered herself bound to them by the same ties which bound her to her other subjects in the Empire, that the prosperity and happiness of the Indian people was the sole aim of her rule, and that everything in India would be freely and equally open to all without distinction of race, or colour, or creed. It is true that in practice this equality has been a mere legal fiction. But then even as a legal fiction it was a very important thing as laying down in theory the policy of a great nation towards a subject people. Now Lord Curzon, who dearly loves debating, thought it proper to attack the educated classes in regard to their constant reference to this Proclamation. He said in effect: "You base your claim for equality on the Queen's Proclamation. But what does it promise you? It says that you will have equality when you are 'qualified' for it. Now, here we have certain qualifications which can only be attained by heredity or race. Therefore, as you cannot acquire race, you really cannot have equality with Englishmen in India as long as British rule lasts."

Now, apart from the question of your national honour being involved in this—the explaining away of a Sovereign's word—look at the unwisdom, the stupendous unwisdom, of the whole thing—telling the people of India that, unless they were content to remain permanently a subject race in their own country, their interests and those of British rule were not identical. After this, how can any Englishman complain if my countrymen regarded, as they have been latterly regarding, your rule in India as maintained, not to promote their interests, but for a selfish purpose? But Lord Curzon has not stopped even at this. Some time ago he made a speech in Convocation at Calcutta, in which he attacked not only the educated classes of to-day, but also their ancestors of whom he knows nothing, and the ideals of their race, of which every Indian is justly proud.

And then on the top of these things has come the partition of Bengal. Ladies and gentlemen, I don't wish to say anything tonight about the merits of the measure, now that it has been carried out. I regret it profoundly. I think it has been a terrible mistake and it will take long to undo its evil effects, if ever you are able to undo them. But I want to say a word about the manner in which [the] measure has been forced on that province. About two years ago Lord Curzon started the idea; and instantly there was strenuous opposition to it throughout the province. About 500 meetings were held in different parts in which the people begged Lord Curzon to leave them alone. For a time nothing more was heard of the proposal, and people thought Lord Curzon had abandoned the partition. A few months ago it was suddenly announced, not only that the partition would take place, but that a much larger scheme than was originally proposed had been sanctioned by the Secretary of State. Now, consider the position. The people had held 500 meetings, they had appealed to the Viceroy, they had appealed to the Secretary of State, they had sent a petition signed by 60,000 persons, to the British House of Commons; and yet, in spite of all these things, this measure had been forced upon the people. The Lieutenant-Governor of Bengal says that he had consulted his senior officials, as if they were the only people to be consulted in a matter of this kind! No Indians were consulted, not even the men who never take part in politics, who are the friends of Viceroys and the Lieutenant-Governors, heads of distinguished families—not one even of these was consulted; and you find all these men ranged against the partition to-day. Now, is this the way British rule is to be maintained in India after a hundred years? It is this which has driven the people of Bengal to the present feeling of despair. The majority of the people there have lost faith in the character of your rule, and that to my mind is a serious situation.

Now though the main part of the responsibility for this state of things must rest on Lord Curzon, after all it is your system of administration in India that has enabled him to attempt all this repression. My quarrel, therefore, is less with him personally, or with the officials, than with the system—this bureaucratic system, this monopoly of power by officials. Many of these officials are, no doubt, conscientious men, who are trying to do their duty according to their lights. But I contend that these lights are dim. Their highest idea of British rule is efficiency. They think that if they give India an efficient administration the whole of their work is discharged. But this really is not the whole duty, nor even the main duty, which England has professed to undertake in India. But you have pledged your word before God and man to so govern India as to enable the Indian people to govern themselves according to the higher standards of the West. If your policy is not directed to this end, I shall consider you have failed. I recognize the enormous difficulties but I say, for one thing, your faces should be set in one direction and one direction only, and there must be no attempt at turning back. Again, even as regards efficiency, my own conviction is that it is impossible for the present system to produce more than a certain very limited amount of efficiency; and that standard has now been already reached. The higher efficiency, which comes of self-government, that you can never secure under a bureaucratic system. There are obvious disadvantages inseparable from the system.

I will mention only three of them. In the first place, there is nobody in the government who is permanently identified with the interests of the people. It is a strongly centralised system, and all initiation of important measures can only come from the centre. The centre, however, consists of men who only hold power for five years, and then come away here. It is impossible for them to study vast and complicated problems affecting three hundred millions of people and attempt to deal with them during their time. And when they come away, other men who take their place have to begin where they did, and are deterred by the same difficulty. The Civil Service, taken as a body, is very strong, but each member of it individually is not important enough, owing to the centralised character of the system, to be able to initiate any large measure. Then, as soon as these men have earned their pension, they return to this country. And thus the knowledge and experience acquired by them at the expense of the country—which might have been useful to the people after their retirement, if they had remained in India—is wholly lost to the country, and this goes on generation after generation. When these men come back to this country, they get lost in the crowd, their knowledge and experience finding, perhaps, occasional expression in a letter to the newspapers. The result is that large questions affecting the welfare of the people are generally left to themselves—we, who are permanently in India, have no voice in the government, and can initiate nothing—and this is the first disadvantage of the system, even from the standpoint of efficiency.

The second disadvantage is that which comes of the exclusion of the educated classes from power. This class is steadily growing, and unless you close your schools, colleges and universities, it will continue to grow. And with the growth of this class larger and larger grows the number of men who are discontented with the present state of things. Public opinion is practically limited to these men in the first instance, but what they think to-day the whole country thinks to-morrow. And there is no other public opinion in the country. Now, you never can get much efficiency with the whole country in a discontented frame of mind.

Lastly, the officials look at every question from the standpoint of their own power. They jealously guard their own monopoly of power and subordinate every thing to this consideration. The interests of the services are thus allowed to take precedence of the interests of the people. You thus see the revenue of the country eaten up by the enormous and steadily growing military expenditure, the increasing Home Charges, and the extravagant salaries paid to the English officials, while next to nothing is spent on primary education, and industrial education is absolutely neglected. In the old times, when your rule had to be consolidated, and Western standards had to be introduced into the country, your work was done in a manner which secured the gratitude of the people, but that gratitude is, I fear, now over.

The new generation does not know what was done two generations ago. They only know your rule as it now is, and they only see your officials enjoying a monopoly of power and resisting all the legitimate efforts of the people to participate in that power. New generations are thus growing up full of bitterness for the exclusion of which they have every right to complain. They see the marvellous rise of Japan,[12] and they see that, while in Japan the whole weight of the government has been thrown on the side of popular progress, in India the whole weight of the government has been against popular progress. Now I want you to consider whether such a state of things can be indefinitely prolonged. And, after all, though the bureaucracy actually exercises power, it is on you, the people of this country, that the real responsibility for the government of India rests.

I am aware that much good has been done by England in India in certain directions. The Western type of the administrative machinery has been substituted in place of what we once had. The country enjoys now uninterrupted peace and order. Justice, though costly, is fairly dispensed, as between Indian and Indian, though when it comes to be a matter between Indian and Englishman, it is quite another story. Then you have introduced Western education, with freedom of speech and freedom of writing. These are all things that stand to your credit.

Side by side with these there have been great evils. One such evil is a steady dwarfing of the race in consequence of its exclusion from power. Our natural abilities, owing to sheer disuse, are growing less and less; and this stunting is, in my opinion, an enormous evil. Another evil is economic, and there I hold strongly [that] British rule has produced disastrous results. On this point, I claim some right to speak for I have been studying this phase of the question for nearly twenty years now. Now, as a temporary necessity of a state of transition, even these great evils might be borne, though they are undoubtedly most serious. When your bureaucracy attempts to make the present arrangements permanent, the position is simply impossible.

The only solution that is possible—a solution demanded alike by our interests and by your interests, as also by your national honour—is the steady introduction of self-government in India. Substituting the Indian for the English agency, expanding and reforming the Legislative Councils till they become in reality true controlling bodies, and letting the people generally manage their own affairs themselves. The task, though difficult, is not impossible. What is needed is large statesmanship and a resolute determination to see to it that the pledges given to the people of India are redeemed within a reasonable span of time. The bureaucracy, no doubt, will not like to part with power, and will do everything it can to thwart this consummation. But, after all, they are only the servants of the British people, and when you have definitely made up your minds they will be bound to carry out your policy.

VI
BAL GANGADHAR TILAK

> If any one can claim to be truly the father of Indian unrest, it is Bal Gangadhar Tilak.
>
> VALENTINE CHIROL

Introduction

PRIOR TO THE ENTRANCE of Lokamanya Tilak (1856–1920) upon the political stage, Indian leadership afforded the spectacle of a rather polite debating society which accepted British ideals and values as almost axiomatic.[1] Protests against government policies consisted of thoughtfully worded petitions calculated to appeal to the sense of reason and fair play of officials. Tilak saw little profit in such method and ridiculed his rivals in the Nationalist leadership, particularly Gokhale, who were wedded to the traditions of British parliamentary procedure.

As a Chitpawan Brahman, Tilak inherited a tradi-

75

tion of activism in public affairs that dates back at least to the times of the Maratha Confederacy.[2] Like his predecessors in Maharashtra politics, he believed in an active life for the Brahman community. He insisted, "Religion and practical life are not different . . . Make the country your family instead of working only for your own. The step beyond it is to serve humanity and the next step is to serve God." [3]

Tilak's first public activities revolved about Poona's New English School, of which he was the co-founder in 1880. The educational program was designed to bring a high quality of instruction to the Indian population, in order to provide an intelligent popular basis for the rebirth of the Indian nation. The amazing success of the school, which in four years surpassed in matriculation results all other schools in the Bombay Presidency, was due chiefly to the ability and dedication of the founders, of whom the Lokamanya was probably the ablest.[4]

In 1884, Tilak and his colleagues formed the famous Deccan Education Society which proceeded to establish Fergusson College, in Poona, the following year. This institution attempted to provide the type of education essential to a new generation of Nationalist leaders in India—an education free of European points of view, yet using Western knowledge as well as Sanskrit learning. It was in the Deccan Education Society that the Lokamanya's differences with Gokhale first came to a head, leading to the former's resignation from the society in 1890. Nevertheless, this painful wrench in his life gave Tilak an even more active role in the Indian Nationalist movement, for he turned

from a position in which he was engaged in spreading
the English language and Western science to one where
he could use the Marathi language to rouse the masses
to take pride in their Hindu traditions.

Earlier, a year after the founding of the New
English School, Tilak and five others had established
the *Mahratta* and the *Kesari* newspapers, the former
published in English and the latter in Marathi. Both
journals aimed at the education of the Hindu population of Western India, the *Kesari*, or "Lion," intended
especially as an organ of mass education and popular
agitation. By 1882, the *Kesari* had a greater circula-
tion than any other Indian vernacular newspaper.
As a result of his editorials, the Lokamanya was to
become involved, more than once, with the British
courts. After his resignation from the Deccan Education Society, he took over complete control and editor-
ship of both newspapers.

His first major public controversy involved the so-
called "Age of Consent Bill." This was a pet program
of Gokhale and the liberal reformers, aimed at prevent-
ing the abuses associated with child marriages. The
Lokamanya's objections to such reform were not so
much to the idea of discouraging early marriage as
to the use of compulsion by the British Government
in the sphere of Hindu domestic customs. He himself
had postponed the marriage of his own daughters, but
he believed that legal measures should be invoked
only by Indians themselves, after the attainment of
self-government. The reform element won out, however, and the bill became law in the Bombay Presidency. But by his vigorous opposition to the move-

ment Tilak had become a spokesman for orthodox Maratha Hindus.[5]

To further strengthen Indian consciousness of and pride in Hindu traditions, the Lokamanya was instrumental in establishing festivals to the deity, Ganapati, and to Shivaji, symbol of Maratha power and glory. These and other activities, supported largely through vigorous editorials in the *Kesari* and stirring speeches in village and city alike, brought Tilak a steadily increasing weight of popular support and placed him under growing suspicion by British officials.

The Lokamanya's philosophy was bound to bring him into conflict with others in the Congress, as it had earlier in the Deccan Education Society, and with the same elements. The climax of this struggle occurred in 1907, during the famous "Surat Split." Tilak was the leader of the Nationalist wing of the Congress Party, and at the annual meeting he and his followers insisted on the drafting of resolutions stressing self-government, national education, and the use of the boycott. Arguments over the resolutions, and a furious melee on the floor during the second day of the meeting, resulted in the moderate Reform wing of the party seizing control of the convention. Tilak and the Nationalists thereupon walked out of the Congress.[6]

This hopeless impasse with the moderates is well illustrated by his comments after the Surat Split: "Besides the ordinary Swadeshi movement, we work by boycott and passive resistance . . ."[7] And in passive resistance we shall simply refuse to notice such measures as the Seditious Meeting Act; but we do not care what happens to ourselves. We are devoted to the cause of the Indian peoples . . . That is our object—to attract the attention of England to our wrongs by diverting trade and obstructing the government . . ." [8]

It was not until 1916 that Tilak returned to the Congress. Meanwhile he suffered six years of imprisonment in Mandalay, for sedition. He died August 1, 1920, the day that Gandhi inaugurated the national Noncoöperation movement.

The brief excerpted passages from his writings and speeches that follow have been chosen from different periods of his life, but together they reveal his persistent theme of Swaraj, despite the more moderate tone apparent in what he had to say in later years.

Swaraj
BY BAL GANGADHAR TILAK

[The year 1907:] This alien Government has ruined the country. In the beginning, all of us were taken by surprise. We were almost dazed. We thought that everything that the rulers did was for our good and that this English Government had descended from the clouds to save us from the invasions of Tamerlane and Genghis Khan, and, as they say, not only from foreign invasions

79

but from internecine warfare, or the internal or external invasions, as they call it. We felt happy for a time, but it soon came to light that the peace which was established in this country did this, as Mr. Dadabhai[9] has said in one place—that we were prevented from going at each other's throats, so that a foreigner might go at the throats of us all. *Pax Britannica* has been established in this country in order that a foreign Government may exploit the country. That this is the effect of this *Pax Britannica* is being gradually realised in these days. It was an unhappy circumstance that it was not realized sooner.

Mr. Dadabhai at the age of 82 tells us that he is bitterly disappointed. Mr. Gokhale, I know, is not disappointed. He is a friend of mine and I believe that this is his honest conviction. Mr. Gokhale is not disappointed but is ready to wait another 80 years till he is disappointed like Mr. Dadabhai. There is no empire lost by a free grant of concessions by the rulers to the ruled. History does not record any such event. Empires are lost by luxury, by being too much bureaucratic or overconfident or from other reasons. But an empire has never come to an end by the rulers conceding power to the ruled.

You got the Queen's Proclamation.[10] But it was obtained without a Congress. They wanted to pacify you, as you had grown too turbulent, and you got that Proclamation without a demand, without Congress and without constitutional agitation.

The educated classes alone have the knowledge and the courage for agitation and naturally the State Secretary treats them as enemies. But I appeal to you that the educated classes need not despair over such a thing. The educated classes are no doubt poor but they have one compensating advantage. They possess knowledge, and knowledge is not poor inasmuch as it possesses unlimited potentiality for wealth of every sort. They may also rely upon gradually bringing to their side those classes on whose support Government now thinks it may rely. History abounds in cases of kingdoms undone by the discontent of penniless beggars. No one could be more poor than the great Chanakya of mediaeval Indian History, and it is well known how Chanakya, who had no stake in the world but the little knot of his hair, exterminated the whole race of the Nandas in return for the insult that was desperately given to him.[11] Mr. Morley of all persons should not have scorned the power of educated men because they were poor and had no earthly stake.[12] But when thoughtful men like Mr. Morley betray such evident signs of thoughtlessness, then surely the decline of the British Raj has begun . . .

Mr. Paranjpe and another speaker have referred to the theory of social contract of Rousseau, and Mr. Damale has construed the Proclamation of 1858 as a contract.[13] For my part I think that the word "contract" cannot be made applicable to relations existing between unequals, and it is dangerous for us to be deluded into a belief that the Proclamation is anything like a contract. No doubt it was a pledge solemnly given, but in its inception it was an utterance made in only a statesmanly spirit, because it was calculated to make for peace at the time. But the finger of the tactician is discernible in it.

It is essentially an English idea that a political agitation is an attempt to enforce the terms of such an agreement. The Eastern idea is different; but it is a mistake to hold that it does not warrant an agitation by the subjects to control the power of the King. The idea is no doubt true that the King is part and parcel of the Godhead, and some foolish people have tried to fling it in the face of the Indian people to detract from their demand for popular institutions. But the canons of interpretation of a text are not less important than the text itself, and the real mischief arises from not construing the text in this respect as it should be. The King or Sovereign is no doubt a part and parcel of the Godhead, but according to the Vedanta, so is every member of the subject people. For is not every soul a chip from the same block of Brahman? It is absurd to suppose that the Indian lawgivers of old regarded a King as absolved from all duties towards his subjects. Why, Manu has distinctly laid down, for instance, that the King who punishes those whom he should not, or does not punish those whom he should, goes to hell.[14]

And the beauty of it is that this penalty is not stipulated for in an agreement or contract but is imposed by the Rishis, that is to say, those who were absolutely disinterested in wordly affairs and to whom, therefore, the sacred work of legislation fell. The Hindu believes in a multiplicity of "Devatas" or deities, and we all know what happens to the King that becomes undutiful. The King may himself be a sort of deity, but the conflict between him and his subjects begets another deity superior to him. And if the cause of the people be just, the second deity quietly absorbs the first. It is well known that both Parashurama and Rama are regarded as direct in- carnations of God.[15] But it is on record that when the days of the sixth incarnation were numbered the flame of glory and power, as the Purana graphically describes it, came out from the mouth of Parashurama and entered that of Rama. And what was Parashurama but a mere human being when he was deprived of this flame, the insignia of divinity? This divine ele- ment in kingship even according to Oriental ideas is not free from its peculiar limitations, and I challenge any one to point out any text which lays down that the yoke of the tyranny of a ruler, whoever he may be, should be quietly borne. The divine King as soon as he ceases to be just ceases also to be divine. He be- comes an "Asura" and this depreciated divinity is forthwith replaced by a deity, the divinity in which is not so alloyed.[16]

But then it may be urged, that we shall have to suffer for doing what I want you to do. But then, the path of duty is never sprinkled with rosewater, nor do roses grow on it. It is true that what we seek may seem like a revolution in the sense that it means a com- plete change in the "theory" of the Government of India as now put forward by the bureaucracy. It is true that this revolution must be a bloodless revolu- tion, but it would be a folly to suppose that if there is to be no shedding of blood there are also to be no sufferings to be undergone by the people. Why, even these sufferings must be great. But you can win nothing unless you are prepared to suffer. The war between selfishness and reason, if it is conducted only with the weapons of syllogism, must result in the victory for the former, and an appeal to the good feelings of the rulers is everywhere discovered to have but narrow limits. Your revolution must be bloodless; but that does not mean that you may not have to suffer or to go to jail.

Your fight is with bureaucracy who will always try to curb and suppress you. But you must remember that consistently with the spirit of laws and the bloodlessness of the revolution, there are a hundred other means by which you may and ought to achieve your object, which is to force the hands of the bureaucracy to concede the reforms and privileges demanded by the people. You must realise that you are a great factor in the power with which the administration in India is conducted. You are yourselves the useful lubricants which enable the gigantic machinery to work so smoothly.

Though down-trodden and neglected, you must be conscious of your power of making the administration impossible if you but choose to make it so. It is you who manage the railroad and the telegraph, it is you who make settlements and collect revenues, it is in fact you who do everything for the administration though in a subordinate capacity. You must consider whether you cannot turn your hand to better use for your nation than drudging on in this fashion. Let your places be filled by Europeans on the splendid salary of eight annas a day if possible! You must seriously consider whether your present conduct is self-respectful to yourselves or useful to the nation.

You must also consider what humiliation you have to suffer when foreigners openly express their wonder at the three hundred millions of Indians bearing their present ignominious lot without any effective protest. To say this, is not to violate the spirit of laws of any constitution. Surely it does not violate the sense of God's justice as we understand it. It is but those who oppose the reasonable demands of the Indian people that offend against God's justice.

[The year 1908:] When one country rules over another, the principal aim of the rulers is self-interest alone; but the extent of such self-interest is bounded in such a way that the subjects might not get exasperated. What is called statesmanship consists only in this; and this very thing has been designated enlighted self-interest by some English authors. British rule in India has been carried on on this very principle, but the great mistake that is being committed is that the English official class does not at all take the advice or opinion of the subjects or their leaders in the matter of our administration. The whole problem of the welfare of subjects has been taken by the white official class in its own hands. And they are vain enough to think in this wise: "Whatever thing we might do or whatever policy we might decide upon in the light of our wisdom or enlightened self-interest, must alone be uncomplainingly accepted as beneficial to themselves by the people of India and they must invoke a blessing upon us for the same."

But owing to the spread of Western education, it is not now possible for this condition to last any longer.

85

However enlightened the self-interest of the rulers might be, India must still be a loser thereby; and in order to prevent this loss the power in the hands of the white official class must gradually come into our hands; there is no other alternative; such is now the view of many people in India and it is gaining ground. Such an impression being ultimately injurious to the ruling official class, the white official class here has become eager to suppress completely the writings, speeches or other means which produce that impression. If they had been able to drive the car of the entire administration solely according to their own views, many oppressive enactments like the Prevention of Seditious Meetings Act would by this time have been passed, and India would fully have become another Russia. But the experience gained from history, democratic public opinion in England and the awakening caused throughout the whole continent of Asia by the rise of an Oriental nation like that of Japan have come in the way of the oppressive policy of our white official class and have imposed some restrictions on their imperial autocratic sway.[17]

However, the desire of the people gradually to obtain the rights of Swaraj is growing stronger and stronger, and if they do not get rights by degrees, as desired by them, then some people at least out of the subject population, being filled with indignation or exasperation, will not fail to embark upon the commission of improper or horrible deeds recklessly. The Honourable Mr. Gokhale himself has, in the course of one of his speeches in the Supreme Legislative Council, given a hint of this very kind to our

Government in the presence of the Viceroy. When Lala Lajpat Rai was deported [18] without trial and the proclamation about prevention of meetings promulgated, other native editors of newspapers also, like ourselves, plainly gave the Government to understand that if they resorted in that manner to oppressive Russian methods then the Indian subjects, too, would be compelled to imitate, partially at least, the methods of Russian subjects! "As you sow, so you reap" is a well-known maxim. For rulers to tell their subjects "We shall practise whatever oppression we like, deport any one we choose without trial, partition any province we like, stop any meeting we choose, or prosecute any one we like for sedition and send him to jail, but you, on your part, should silently endure all those things and should not allow your indignation, exasperation or vehemence to go beyond certain limits," is to show the world that they do not know common human nature.

Most of the Anglo-Indian newspaper editors have committed this very mistake when writing on the Muzaffarpur affair. [19] They have brought a charge against the Indian leaders that it was by the very writings or speeches of the said leaders who passed severe comments on the high-handed or contumacious conduct of the English official class, that the present terrible situation was brought about. They have next made a recommendation that Government should henceforth place greater restrictions upon the speeches, writings or movements of these leaders. In our opinion, this suggestion is most silly. Just as when a dam built across a river begins to give way owing to the flood

caused by excessive rain, the blame for the mishap
should be thrown on the rain and not on the flood,
even so, if in society there is any transgression of legal
bounds in a few cases owing to the discontent or exasperation engendered by the oppressive acts of an
irresponsible and unrestrained official class, the blame
or the responsibility for it must be placed on the policy
of the unrestricted official class alone.

The rule of the autocratic, unrestricted and irresponsible white official class in India is becoming
more and more unbearable to the people. All thoughtful men in India are putting forth efforts in order that
this rule or authority, instead of remaining with the
said official class, should come into the hands of the
representatives of the subject people. Some think that
this thing can be accomplished by supplicating this
intoxicated official class itself, or by petitioning the
Government in England who exercise supervision over
it. Some others think this improbable, and they have
persuaded themselves that, in accordance with the
maxim, 'the mouth does not open unless the nose is
stopped,' unless a spoke is put somewhere into the
wheels of the car of the present rulers, their desired
object will not be accomplished. The opinion of this
party is that whatever may be wanted should be plainly
stated and it should be obtained by following the
path of passive resistance.[20] But to say that not even
a single man out of the thirty crores of people in the
country should go beyond these two paths in the
paroxysm of the indignation or exasperation produced
by this oppressive system of Government, is like saying
that the indignation or exasperation of the thirty

crores of the inhabitants of India must always necessarily remain below a certain degree.

[The year 1914:] I find that during the six years of my
absence an attempt has been made in the English Press
here and in England, as for example in Mr. Chirol's
book, to interpret my actions and writings as a direct
or indirect incitement to deeds of violence, or my
speeches as uttered with the object of subverting the
British rule in India.[21] I am sorry the attempt happened to be made at a time when I was not a free citizen
to defend myself. But I think I ought to take the first
public opportunity to indignantly repudiate these
nasty and totally unfounded charges against me. I
have, like other political workers, my own differences
with the Government as regards certain measures and
to a certain extent even the system of internal administration. But it is absurd on that account to speak
of my actions or my attitude as in any way hostile to
His Majesty's Government. That has never been my
wish or my object. I may state once for all that we are
trying in India, as the Irish Homerulers have been
doing in Ireland, for a reform of the system of administration and not for the overthrow of Government;
and I have no hesitation in saying that the acts of
violence which have been committed in the different
parts of India are not only repugnant to me, but
have, in my opinion, only unfortunately retarded to
a great extent, the pace of our political progress.
Whether looked at from an individual or from a
public point of view they deserve, as I have said
before on several occasions, to be equally condemned.

It has been well said that British Rule is conferring inestimable benefit on India not only by its civilized methods of administration but also thereby bringing together the different nationalities and races of India, so that a united Nation may grow out of it in course of time. I do not believe that if we had any other rulers except the liberty-loving British, they could have conceived and assisted us in developing such a National Ideal. Everyone who has the interest of India at heart is fully alive to this and similar advantages of the British Rule; and the present crisis is, in my opinion, a blessing in disguise inasmuch as it has universally evoked our united feelings and sentiments of loyalty to the British Throne.

[The year 1916:] No one asks you to obtain your rights by the use of the sword. To-day the nation's mind has undergone a change. India can give some help to England. If India be happy England too will acquire a sort of glory, a sort of strength and a sort of greatness. This consciousness has been awakened in England. If no advantage is taken of this awakened consciousness at this time, such an opportunity will not occur again. The bureaucracy considers this to be bad. Who will be the loser in this? Not the Emperor, but the bureaucracy. They, therefore, consider this thing to be bad, and they are now telling us that we are not fit for Swaraj and that, therefore, they have come here. As if there was no Swaraj anywhere in India when they were not here. We all were barbarians and ready to cut each other's throats. There was no system of administration under the Peshwa's regime.[22]

Swaraj

There was no system of administration under the Mohammedan regime. We were not able to carry on State
administration, we were not able to construct roads.
We did not know how the people might be happy.
Nana Phadnavis was a fool, Malik Amber was a fool,
Akbar and Aurangzeb were fools.[23] Therefore these
people have come here for our good and we are still
children. Let us admit for a moment also that we are
children. When are we to become grown up?

We want freedom. We must have in our hands the
right of carrying on our affairs. If you do not get these
things, no reform will be fruitful to you. That is the
root of all reforms. Do you believe that the people
who have come to rule over us are superiors to us in
intelligence and learning? Such is not my own belief.
We can show as much learning, as much courage, as
much ability as they. Perhaps they may not be apparent now, but they are in us. There are conjunctions
in history as well as in astronomy. When the Mohammedan rule was declining, the Marathas had only
recently risen. Afterwards, the English having set
foot in India, the whole power passed into their
possession, and their power is the cause of the admiration which we feel for them and the pride—be it
true or false—which we feel for their ability.

The duty which you have is to agitate so that this
administration must be changed. The King need not
be changed. Unless the system—the arrangement according to which the present administration is carried
on—is changed, every man in India will become more
and more effeminate. The duty which we have to
perform is to stop that. Some people say, "What does

it matter if there is slavery? Do they not give us to
eat? They do not starve any one to death." Even the
beast and the birds get to eat. To get to eat is not
the aim of man. To feed the family is not the end of
man. Even a crow lives and eats offerings. A crow
maintains itself. I do not consider it manliness merely
to maintain oneself and fill the belly, to obey the
commands of the administration, accepting posts
which may be kept open within the limits laid down
by it, and to maintain oneself according to its direction. This docile nature is common to beasts and
men. If there is required the quality of manhood in
man, then we should see whether there is any scope
open for our intellect, our ability, our courage and
boldness. Such scope is not open in India. Therefore,
if we have any duty to perform, then the first duty
is to take a portion of this authority into our possession.

[The year 1917:] Those that hold power in their
hands at present imagine that Indians are not capable
of governing themselves to the limited extent implied
by the word Home Rule. They do not tell Indians
when they will be able to govern themselves. They
do not fix any time-limit. Once it used to be said that
Asiatic nations were not fit for self-government. That
however is not said now. They now say that India is
not *now* fit for self-government. If Indians ask them
why, they are told that they are deficient in education,
there are numerous castes quarrelling among themselves, and only British administrators can hold the
balance even between rival sections.

What is unfitness? Do they mean to say that before the British came here there was no peaceful rule anywhere in India? What was Akbar? Was he a bad ruler? No Englishmen can say that. Let them go back to Hindu rule. There were the empires of Asoka, the Guptas, the Rajputs, etc. No history could say that all these empires had managed their states without any system of administration. There were empires in India as big as the German empire and the Italian empire and they were governed peacefully. When peace reigned in the country under the Hindu, Buddhist and Mohammedan rules, what ground is there to say that the descendants of those people who governed those empires are to-day unfit to exercise that right? There is no disqualification, intellectual or physical, which disables them from taking part in the Government of any empire. They have shown their fitness in the past and are prepared to show it to-day if opportunities are granted to them. The charge of unfitness comes only from those who hold the monopoly of power in their hands. In every case of monopoly that argument is used. The East India Company used that argument. None of us whose ancestors founded and administered empires would subscribe to the doctrine that Indians, whether Hindus or Moslems, are incapable of governing themselves. The charge of incapacity is only brought forward by interested people, because self-interest demands that some argument must be advanced in their support.

We are not given higher posts to show our capacity. We are only given subordinate posts. Without the aid

of Indians in the subordinate departments it would
be impossible for the British people to carry on the
administration; and so we are given all the subordinate posts. We have been fighting ever since the
establishment of the Congress to break this monopoly
and not without success. A few posts reserved for the
civil service have been granted to us. A few appointments in the judicial department—High Court judge-
ships, etc.—have been granted to us. What is the
result? I have not seen any resolution of the Government saying that when any post of responsibility is
given to Indians they have misused those opportunities, that they have failed to come up to the standard
of efficiency required. On the contrary, resolutions
have been issued saying that Indians who have acted
as members of executive councils have done their
duty very well. If one went to the Indian States one
would find that all higher posts are held by Indians.
What do the British administration reports say about
these States? They say that they are well administered.
So the whole evidence is in our favour. After barring
us from the higher services, saying that we are not
capable of governing is adding insult to injury. This
kind of jugglery will not do. The British democracy
will not tolerate it. If we simply press the right view
on the British public, they will hear it now because
they are in a mood to hear it. We have logic and
experience on our side, but mere logic and truth will
not succeed in this world unless backed up by persistent agitation and a fixed determination to attain
that truth. We must be determined to see that truth
triumphs and that triumph is what we mean to

achieve. The Home Rule agitation is intended for that purpose.

Whatever that be, one thing is certain, that the work before us is not easy. Tremendous sacrifices will be necessary; nay, we shall have to tide over it; there are two ways of dying, one constitutional and the other unconstitutional. As our fight is going to be constitutional and legal, our death also must, as of necessity, be constitutional and legal. We have not to use any violence. Nay, we condemn the unconstitutional way of doing. As our fight must be constitutional it must be courageous also.

We ought to tell Government courageously and without the least fear what we want. Let Government know that the whole Nation wants Home Rule, as defined by the Congress. Let there be no shirking, or wavering, or shaking. I said that it was our "right" to have Home Rule but that is a historical and a European way of putting it; I go further and say that it is our "Dharma"; you cannot separate Home Rule from us, as you cannot separate the quality of "heat" from fire; both are inseparably bound up;[24] let your ideas be clear; let your motives be honest; let your efforts be strictly constitutional and I am sure your efforts are bound to be crowned with success; never despair, be bold and fearless and be sure that God is with you. Remember "God helps those who help themselves."

VII

LALA LAJPAT RAI

Lalaji means an institution. From his youth, he made
of his country's service a religion. Men like him
cannot die as long as the sun shines in the Indian
sky. His love of service was insatiable.

M. K. GANDHI

Introduction

THOSE NATIONALISTS who chose to oppose British rule more or less openly had a choice of three al-
ternatives: parliamentary criticism, jail, exile. Men
like Ranade and Gokhale chose the first; Tilak,
Gandhi, and Nehru courted the second; Lala Lajpat
Rai (1865–1921) followed the third course. To say
that some enjoyed the freedom and dignity of official
debate while others languished in prison or exile is
not to condemn the former as cowardly nor to praise
the latter unduly for courage. Each of the Congress

leaders managed to apply his talents in the effective and appropriate area. None could have played Gokhale's part in the councils with such patience and with such far-reaching influence. Nor could Gokhale have functioned as successfully as Lajpat Rai in the role of public hero.

Like Tilak, Lajpat Rai was an orator, dominating the Punjab as Tilak did the Maharashtra. A contemporary described him thus: "As a public speaker, I think of Lloyd George and Lajpat Rai together. They had equal capacity for rousing the indignation of the masses. I have heard few speeches which would be placed by the side of Lajpat Rai's speeches in Urdu in the thrilling effect they produced upon the mass mind. Some of his Urdu speeches could only be compared to Mr. Lloyd George's orations at Limehouse and Mile End . . . The subject was the position of Indians in South Africa . . . Gokhale and Pandit Malaviya were followed by Lala Lajpat Rai in a speech in Urdu, and he aroused the passions of the people with such intensity by a speech so masculine that I thought at the time that if any South Africans were anywhere within striking distance his life would not be safe." [1]

In 1905 Lajpat Rai was sent as a member of a delegation to England, to present Indian grievances on behalf of the Indian National Congress. His vigorous attacks upon British policies brought him unavoidably into disfavor with the government. As a result, he was exiled in 1907, and later he made his home in the United States, from 1914 to 1919. During this time he wrote and published various books and

97

articles in defense of India and of Hindu culture, writings highly critical of the British and of Western civilization in general.[2]

His deportation made him a national hero. When he returned he was the unanimous choice for president of the special session of the Congress which met at Calcutta in 1920. Despite some earlier opposition to Gandhian theories of Noncoöperation, he gave the movement his full support when it was launched that same year.[3] In 1922 he was imprisoned, and in 1928 he died, following a beating administered by government police during a boycott demonstration at Lahore.[4]

He was devoted to many charitable, political, and social projects and became the leader of the Arya Samaj, a Hindu traditionalist movement. He edited a vernacular magazine and a weekly journal. But his great interest was in the education of youth. He founded the Dayananda Anglo-Vedic College, and in order to train national leaders, he established the Tilak School of Politics at Lahore, endowing it chiefly from his own funds. Lajpat Rai's comments (1919) on the Montagu-Chelmsford Report, in the article that follows, is typical of his vigorous journalism.

The Remedy for Revolution

BY LALA LAJPAT RAI

The authors of the Montagu-Chelmsford report remark:[5]

> There exists a small revolutionary party deluded
> by hatred of British rule and desire for the
> elimination of the Englishman into the belief
> that the path to independence or constitutional
> liberty lies through anarchical crime. Now it may
> be that such persons will see for themselves the
> wisdom of abandoning methods which are as
> futile as [they are] criminal; though if they do
> not, the powers of the law are or can be made
> sufficient for the maintenance of order. But the
> existence of such people is a warning against the
> possible consequences of unrestrained agitation
> in India. We are justified in calling on the
> political leaders, in the work of education that
> they will undertake, to bear carefully in mind
> the political inexperience of their hearers; and
> to look for further progress not to fiery agitation
> which may have consequences quite beyond their
> grasp, but to the machinery which we devise for

99

the purpose. In every country there will be persons who love agitation for agitation's sake or
to whom it appeals like an intoxicant. It is the
duty of the leaders of Indian opinion to remember the effect on people not accustomed to weigh-
ing words of fiery and heated speeches. Where
ignorance is wide-spread and passions are so
easily aroused, nothing is easier than for political
leaders to excite a storm; nothing harder for
them than to allay it. Breaches of the peace or
crimes of violence only put back the political
clock.

We are in general agreement with the sentiments
expressed in this extract but we will be wanting in
candour if we fail to point out that, though the
revolutionary movement in India is mainly political,
it is partly economic and partly anarchic also. In the
first two aspects it is at present the product of purely
local (Indian) conditions. In the last, it is the reaction
of world forces. While we are hoping that the change
in the policy, now announced, will remove the political
basis of it, we are not quite sure that that will ensure the
extermination of the party or the total destruction of
the movement. The growth of democratic political
institutions in India must inevitably be followed by a
movement for social democracy. The spirit of Revolution which is now fed by political inequalities will,
when these are removed, find its sustenance in social
inequalities. That movement may not be anti-British;
perhaps it will not be, but that it will have some
revolutionary element in it may be assumed.

The Remedy for Revolution

The lessons of history make it clear that the most effective way to prevent its falling into channels of violence is to have as little recourse to coercion as may be consistent with the preservation of general order and peace. The preservation of order and the unhindered exercise of private rights by all citizens is the pre-requisite condition to good government. Every government must see to it. It is their duty to use preventive as well as punitive methods. There are, however, ways of doing these things. One is the British, the American and the French way. The other is what was heretofore associated with the name of the late Czar. The third is the German way. We hope the lessons of Czarism will not be lost on either party. The governments have as much to learn from it as the peoples. The best guarantee against the abnormal growth of a revolutionary movement is to adopt and follow the British methods and to avoid scrupulously and without fail any approach to the discredited Russian or Prussian methods.

The Indian soil and the Indian atmosphere are not very congenial for revolutionary ideas and revolutionary methods. The people are too docile, gentle, law-abiding and spiritually inclined to take to them readily. They are by nature and tradition neither vindictive nor revengeful. Their general spirit is opposed to all kinds of violence. They have little faith in the virtues of force. Unless they are provoked, and that too terribly, and are face to face with serious danger they do not like the use of force, even when recourse to it may be legal and morally defensible.

One of the causes of the growth of the revolu-

tionary movement in India has been the insolence
and the incivility of the European Community towards
the Indian Community. The charges of cowardice so
often hurled against the Bengali have played no
insignificant part in the genesis of the Bengal revolutionary. The distinguished authors have put it rather
mildly:

> If there are Indians who really desire to see India
> leave the empire, to get rid of English officers and
> English commerce, we believe that among their
> springs of action will be found the bitterness of
> feeling that has been nurtured out of some mani-
> festation that the Englishman does not think
> the Indian an equal. Very small seeds casually
> thrown may result in great harvests of political
> calamity. We feel that, particularly at the present
> stage of India's progress, it is the plain duty of
> every Englishman and woman, official and non-
> official, in India to avoid the offence and the
> blunder of discourtesy; and none the less is it
> incumbent on the educated Indian to cultivate
> patience and a more generous view of what may
> very likely be no more than heedlessness or
> difference of custom.

We admire the dignified way in which they have
addressed their advice to the educated Indian. But
we hope they do not ignore that except in a few
scattered instances heretofore the chief fault has lain
with the ruling class. The proceedings of the Royal
Commission on the Public Services of India are full
of that racial swagger which the authors of this report

The Remedy for Revolution

have mildly condemned in the above extract and it is an open secret that that spirit was one of the dearly cherished articles of faith with the bureaucracy.[6] We hope the war has effected a great change in their temper and both parties will be disposed to profit from the advice given to them in the report.

As to the duty of the educated leaders in the matter of suppressing the growth of the revolutionary movement in future, we beg to point out that all depends on how much faith the governing classes place in the professions of the popular leaders. Open public speeches and meetings appealing to racial or religious animosities have not played any important part in the development of the revolutionary spirit. It is not likely that the educated leaders will in any way consciously and voluntarily digress from the limits of reasonable criticism of Government policy, nor have they very often done so in the past.

What has so far prevented the educated leaders from exercising an effective check on the growth of the revolutionary movement is their inability to associate on terms of friendship with the younger generation. This has been due partly to a false idea of dignity and partly to the fear that any association with hot-headed young men might bring discredit on them or might land them in hot water if, sometime or other, any one of their friends might do anything violent. Public speeches denouncing the revolutionary propaganda and the revolutionary activities or public condemnation of the latter in the press are good in their own way, but they are not quite effective. The revolutionist may ascribe it to fear, timidity, or hypocrisy. What

is needed is that educated leaders of influence should
be free to mix, socially and otherwise, with the
younger generation so as to acquire an intimate knowledge of their trend of thought and bent of mind. It
is in these intimate exchanges of views that they can
most effectively exercise their powers of argument and
persuasion and use their influence effectively. They
will not succeed always, but in a good many cases
they will. This cannot be done, however, unless the
Executives and the Police relax their attentions toward
them.

The bureaucrats' want of confidence in any Indian
leader reached its limit in the attentions which the
agents of the secret service bestowed on such men as
the late Mr. Gokhale. It is an open secret that the
secret service records have assigned a particular number to every public leader in India. Religious preachers
and teachers of the type of Lala Hansraj and Lala
Munishi Ram receive as much attention in the records
as the writer of this book or Mr. B. G. Tilak or Mr.
Bepin Chandra Pal.[7] The "Servants of India" are as
much the objects of solicitation on the part of the
secret service men as the members of the Arya Samaj.
Of course, agitators are agitators. All the great progressive souls of the world have had to agitate at one
time or another in their lives. Agitation is the soul of
democracy. There can be no progress in a democracy
without agitation.

Sir Denzil Ibbetson could pay no greater compli-
ment to the Arya Samaj than by his remark in 1907
that, according to his information, wherever there was
an Arya Samaj it was a centre of unrest.[8] We hope the

The Remedy for Revolution

Governments are now convinced that the Arya Samaj has never been revolutionary. It is one of the most conservative, restraining forces in the social life of the country. Yet it cannot be denied that its propaganda has been and will continue to be one of the most disturbing factors in the placid waters of Indian life. The bureaucracy could not look upon it with kindness. Any attempt to persist in this kind of control or check or persecution will be fatal to the success of the appeal which Mr. Montagu and Lord Chelmsford have addressed to the public men of India in the extract given above.

In our judgment the most effective way to check the growth of the revolutionary movement is by freeing the mind of the leaders of the fear of being misunderstood if they should mix freely with the younger generation and yet fail to prevent some of them from becoming revolutionists. A revolutionary prospers on exclusiveness. Secrecy is his great ally. Cut off a young man from open, healthy influences and he will be attracted by the mystery of secrecy. Thenceforth he is doomed. After that he may be weaned only by kindness and friendliness and not by threats or persecution. Most of the youths attracted by revolutionary propaganda have proved to be quite ignorant of the real conditions of their country. No attempt has been made to instruct them in politics. They have been fed on unsound history and unsound politics.

Reactionary imperialism has harmed them more than exaggerated nationalism. They have had few opportunities of discussion with people who could look upon things in right perspective. They could not open their minds to their European teachers. In the few cases in which they did they repented. Somehow or other, the free confidential talks they had with their professors found an entry in the police records. It brought a black mark against their names, to stand and mar their careers forever. The Indian teacher and professor is afraid of discussing politics with them. So they go on unrestrained until the glamour of prospective heroism, by a deed of violence, fascinates one of them and he is led into paths of crimes of a most detestable kind. Unscrupulous advisors lead him toward falsehood, hypocrisy, treachery, treason and crime by dubious methods. One of the things they preach is that morality has nothing to do with politics. They insinuate that the violence of militarism and imperialism can be effectively met and checked only by violence. Poor misguided souls!

They forget that once a youth is led into the ways of falsehood and unscrupulousness he may as easily use it against his friends as against his enemies. If he has no scruples about killing an enemy, he may have none about killing a friend. If he has no scruples about betraying the one, he may have none about betraying the other. Once a man starts toward moral degeneration, even for desirable or patriotic ends, there is no knowing whither his course might take him. The most idealistic young men starting with the highest and purest conceptions of patriotism have been known to fall into the most ignoble methods of attacking first their enemies and then their friends. When they reach that stage of moral corruption they can trust no one, can believe in the honesty of no one. Their one idea of cleverness and efficiency is to conceal their motives from everyone, to give their confidence to no one, to suspect and distrust everyone and to aspire toward the success that consists in imposing upon all.

The remedy against this lies in encouraging an open and frank discussion of politics on the part of the younger generation, with such indulgences as are due to their youth and immaturity of judgment; a systematic teaching of political history in schools and colleges; a free and open intercourse with their teachers on the clearest understanding that nothing said in discussion or in confidence will ever be used either privately or publicly against them, and an equally free and intimate intercourse with the leaders of thought and of public life in the country. These latter must be freed from the attentions of the secret service if it is intended that they should effectually coöperate in counteracting revolutionary propaganda.

Besides, the younger generation must be brought up in habits of manly and open encounter with their adversaries, in a spirit of sport and fair play. Repression, suppression, and suspicion do not provide a congenial climate for the development of these habits and they should be subordinated as much as possible in the present condition of chaotic conflict between social interests and social ideals.

VIII

MOHANDAS KARAMCHAND GANDHI

His revolutionary application of moral and spiritual
principles to group life would never have succeeded
if Gandhi had not been able to assess properly the
political and economic situation in the country and
take requisite action at appropriate and psychological
moments.

J. B. KRIPALANI

Introduction

O F ALL THE LEADERS of the Indian nationalist movement, M. K. Gandhi (1869–1948) is least
susceptible of analysis in point of either theory or
action alone. He did not consider himself a philosopher, yet his ideas have permeated the political and
social life of modern India. Refusing emphatically to
separate thought and practice, he must be considered

not only as a theorist but as a man of action; indeed, his ideas are best expressed by the incidents of his public career.

Born and bred in the Gujarati culture of the Kathiawar area north of Bombay, he was heir to the independent spirit of his people, a sturdy Hindu traditionalism, and no doubt also to the insistence on Nonviolence which characterized the doctrines of the Jain population there. His father, uncle, and grandfather had each served as prime minister in one of the small states of the region. His father was noted for his honesty and political courage. His mother was an intensely devout woman, faithful in Hindu religious observances in spite of weariness and weather. Gandhi's life reflected the ways of both parents.

Following a legal education in London, he went to South Africa in 1893 as representative of an Indian firm. There he soon encountered those complex problems of discrimination and conflict that grew out of the relations between resident Indians and British rulers.

He took the lead in organizing the Natal Indian Congress, named after the organization in India.[1] Propaganda was carried on to inform the world about the plight of South African Indians and to win support for proposed reforms among the peoples of Africa, India and England. During his Natal days he engaged in various legal, political and social activities to ameliorate the conditions of his countrymen, most of whom had emigrated as indentured laborers. Perhaps his most significant experiment was the development of a technique and program of Satyagraha, or

Nonviolent action for the redress of wrongs. He finally left Africa in 1914, on the eve of the First World War.

After a brief stay in England, he returned to India, where he founded his famous Satyagraha Ashram at Ahmedabad in 1915.[2] A code of service and humility was drawn up and compliance was required of all members. The following year, a resolution was introduced into Imperial Legislative Council calling for an end to the indenture system for Indian laborers. Gandhi had begun agitation against the practice in 1894, and he now led an active campaign for government action. More than two decades later, in July, 1917, this movement reached its successful conclusion when the British Government announced the end of indentured emigration from India.

Gandhi's first major campaign on a strictly Indian issue began that same year. The philosophy and techniques of this action, as described in the following pages, were based on his earlier African experiences and were so successful that the incidents serve as an example of "Gandhism" at its best.[3] But later campaigns were not to be won so readily. His career was marked by imprisonment, prolonged self-imposed fast, continual controversy, and even withdrawal from public life. Yet he lived to see the achievement of Indian independence before his life, a testimony to the efficacy of Nonviolence, was ironically ended in 1948 by an assassin's bullet.

Face to Face with Ahimsa

BY MOHANDAS KARAMCHAND GANDHI

Champaran is the land of King Janaka.[4] Just as it abounds in Mango groves, so used it to be full of indigo plantations until the year 1917. The Champaran tenant was bound by law to plant three out of every twenty parts of his land with indigo for his landlord. This system was known as the *tinkathia* system as three *kathas* out of twenty (which makes one acre) had to be planted with indigo. . . . My object was to inquire into the condition of the Champaran agriculturists and understand their grievances against the indigo planters. For this purpose it was necessary that I should meet thousands of the ryots.[5] But I deemed it essential, before starting on my inquiry, to know the planters' side of the case and see the Commissioner of the Division. I sought and was granted appointments with both.

The Secretary of the Planters' Association told me plainly that I was an outsider and that I had no business to come between the planters and their tenants, but if I had any representation to make, I might submit it in writing. I politely told him that I did not regard myself as an outsider, and that I had

111

every right to inquire into the condition of the
tenants if they desired me to do so.

The Commissioner, on whom I called, proceeded to
bully me, and advised me forthwith to leave Tirhut.

I acquainted my co-workers with all this, and told
them that there was a likelihood of Government
stopping me from proceeding further, and that I
might have to go to jail earlier than I had expected,
and that, if I was to be arrested, it would be best that
the arrest should take place in Motihari or if possible
in Bettiah. It was advisable, therefore, that I should
go to those places as early as possible.

Champaran is a district of the Tirhut division and
Motihari is its headquarters. Rajkumar Shukla's place
was in the vicinity of Bettiah, and the tenants belong-
ing to the *kothis*[6] in its neighborhood were the poorest
in the district. Rajkumar Shukla wanted me to see
them and I was equally anxious to do so.

So I started with my co-workers for Motihari the
same day. Babu Gorakh Prasad harboured us in his
home, which became a caravanserai. It could hardly
contain us all. The very same day we heard that about
five miles from Motihari a tenant had been ill-treated.
It was decided that, in company with Babu Dharani-
dhar Prasad, I should go and see him the next morning,
and we accordingly set off for the place on elephant's
back. An elephant, by the way, is about as common in
Champaran as a bullock-cart in Gujarat. We had
scarcely gone half way when a messenger from the
Police Superintendent overtook us and said that the
latter had sent his compliments. I saw what he meant.
Having left Dharanidharbabu to proceed to the origi-

nal destination, I got into the hired carriage which
the messenger had brought. He then served on me a
notice to leave Champaran, and drove me to my place.
On his asking me to acknowledge the service of the
notice, I wrote to the effect that I did not propose to
comply with it and leave Champaran till my inquiry
was finished. Thereupon I received a summons to take
my trial the next day for disobeying the order to leave
Champaran.

I kept awake that whole night writing letters and
giving necessary instructions to Babu Brajkishore Prasad.

The news of the notice and the summons spread like
wildfire, and I was told that Motihari that day witnessed unprecedented scenes. Gorakhbabu's house and
the court house overflowed with men. Fortunately I
had finished all my work during the night and so was
able to cope with the crowds. My companions proved
the greatest help. They occupied themselves with
regulating the crowds, for the latter followed me
wherever I went.

A sort of friendliness sprang up between the officials
—Collector, Magistrate, Police Superintendent—and
myself. I might have legally resisted the notices served
on me. Instead I accepted them all, and my conduct
towards the officials was correct. They thus saw that I
did not want to offend them personally, but that I
wanted to offer civil resistance to their orders. In this
way they were put at ease, and instead of harassing me
they gladly availed themselves of my and my co-
workers' cooperation in regulating the crowds. But it
was an ocular demonstration to them of the fact that

their authority was shaken. The people had for the moment lost all fear of punishment and yielded obedience to the power of love which their new friend exercised.

It should be remembered that no one knew me in Champaran. The peasants were all ignorant. Champaran, being far up north of the Ganges, and right at the foot of the Himalayas in close proximity to Nepal, was cut off from the rest of India. The Congress was practically unknown in those parts. Even those who had heard the name of the Congress shrank from joining it or even mentioning it. And now the Congress and its members had entered this land, though not in the name of the Congress, yet in a far more real sense.

In consultation with my co-workers I had decided that nothing should be done in the name of the Congress. What we wanted was work and not name, substance and not shadow. For the name of the Congress was the *bête noire* of the Government and their controllers—the planters. To them the Congress was a byword for lawyers' wrangles, evasion of law through legal loopholes, a byword for bomb and anarchical crime and for diplomacy and hypocrisy. we had to disillusion them both. Therefore we had decided not to mention the name of the Congress and not to acquaint the peasants with the organization called the Congress. It was enough, we thought, if they understood and followed the spirit of the Congress instead of its letter.

No emissaries had therefore been sent there, openly or secretly, on behalf of the Congress to prepare the ground for our arrival. Rajkumar Shukla was incapable of reaching the thousands of peasants. No political work had yet been done amongst them. The world outside Champaran was not known to them. And yet they received me as though we had been age-long friends. It is no exaggeration, but the literal truth, to say that in this meeting with the peasants I was face to face with God, Ahimsa and Truth.[7]

When I come to examine my title to this realization, I find nothing but my love for the people. And this in turn is nothing but an expression of my unshakable faith in Ahimsa.

That day in Champaran was an unforgettable event in my life and a red-letter day for the peasants and for me.

According to the law, I was to be on my trial, but truly speaking Government was to be on its trial. The Commissioner only succeeded in trapping Government in the net which he had spread for me.

The trial began. The Government pleader, the Magistrate and other officials were on tenterhooks. They were at a loss to know what to do. The Government pleader was pressing the Magistrate to postpone the case. But I interfered and requested the Magistrate not to postpone the case, as I wanted to plead guilty to having disobeyed the order to leave Champaran, and read a brief statement as follows:

> With the permission of the Court I would like to make a brief statement showing why I have taken the very serious step of seemingly dis-

115

obeying the order. In my humble opinion it is a question of difference of opinion between the Local Administration and myself. I have entered the country with motives of rendering humanitarian and national service. I have done so in response to a pressing invitation to come and help the ryots, who urge they are not being fairly treated by the indigo planters. I could not render any help without studying the problem. I have, therefore, come to study it with the assistance, if possible, of the Administration and the planters. I have no other motive, and cannot believe that my coming can in any way disturb public peace and cause loss of life. I claim to have considerable experience in such matters. The Administration, however, have thought differently. I fully appreciate their difficulty, and I admit too that they can only proceed upon information they received. As a lawabiding citizen my first instinct would be, as it was, to obey the order served upon me. But I could not do so without doing violence to my sense of duty to those for whom I have come. I feel that I could just now serve them only by remaining in their midst. I could not, therefore, voluntarily retire. Amid this conflict of duties I could only throw the responsibility of removing me from them on the Administration. I am fully conscious of the fact that a person, holding, in the public life of India, a position such as I do, has to be most careful in setting an example. It is my firm belief that in the complex constitution under which we are living, the only safe and honourable course for a self-respecting man is, in the circumstances such as face me, to do what I have decided to do, that is, to submit without protest to the penalty of disobedience.

I venture to make this statement not in any way in extenuation of the penalty to be awarded against me, but to show that I have disregarded the order served upon me not for want of respect for lawful authority, but in obedience to the higher law of our being, the voice of conscience.

There was now no occasion to postpone the hearing, but as both the Magistrate and the Government pleader had been taken by surprise, the Magistrate postponed judgment. Meanwhile I had wired full details to the Viceroy, to Patna friends, as also to Pandit Madan Mohan Malaviya and others.

Before I could appear before the Court to receive the sentence, the Magistrate sent a written message that the Lieutenant Governor had ordered the case against me to be withdrawn, and the Collector wrote to me saying that I was at liberty to conduct the proposed inquiry, and that I might count on whatever help I needed from the officials. None of us was prepared for this prompt and happy issue.

I called on the Collector, Mr. Heycock. He seemed to be a good man, anxious to do justice. He told me that I might ask for whatever papers I desired to see, and that I was at liberty to see him whenever I liked.

The country thus had its first direct object-lesson in Civil Disobedience. The affair was freely discussed both locally and in the press, and my inquiry got unexpected publicity.

It was necessary for my inquiry that the Government should remain neutral. But the inquiry did not need support from press reporters or leading articles in the press. Indeed the situation in Champaran was so delicate and difficult that over-energetic criticism or highly coloured reports might easily damage the cause which I was seeking to espouse. So I wrote to the editors of the principal papers requesting them not to trouble to send any reporters, as I should send them whatever might be necessary for publication and keep them informed.

I knew that the Government attitude countenancing my presence had displeased the Champaran planters, and I knew that even the officials, though they could say nothing openly, could hardly have liked it. Incorrect or misleading reports, therefore, were likely to incense them all the more, and their ire, instead of descending on me, would be sure to descend on the poor fear-stricken ryots and seriously hinder my search for the truth about the case.

In spite of these precautions the planters engineered against me a poisonous agitation. All sorts of falsehoods appeared in the press about my co-workers and myself. But my extreme cautiousness and my insistence on truth, even to the minutest detail, turned the edge of their sword.

The planters left no stone unturned in maligning Brajkishorebabu, but the more they maligned him, the more he rose in the estimation of the people.

In such a delicate situation as this I did not think

GOPAL KRISHNA GOKHALE

LALA LAJPAT RAI

JAWAHARLAL NEHRU

VINOBA BHAVE

it proper to invite any leaders from other provinces. Pandit Malaviyaji had sent me an assurance that, whenever I wanted him, I had only to send him word, but I did not trouble him. I thus prevented the struggle from assuming a political aspect. But I sent to the leaders and the principal papers occasional reports, not for publication, but merely for their information. I had seen that, even where the end might be political, but where the cause was non-political, one damaged it by giving it a political aspect and helped it by keeping it within its non-political limit. The Champaran struggle was a proof of the fact that disinterested service of the people in any sphere ultimately helps the country politically.

It was not quite possible to carry on the work without money. It had not been the practice hitherto to appeal to the public for money for work of this kind. Brajkishorebabu and his friends were mainly vakils who either contributed funds themselves, or found it from friends whenever there was an occasion.[8] How could they ask the people to pay when they and their kind could well afford to do so? That seemed to be the argument. I had made up my mind not to accept anything from the Champaran ryots. It would be bound to be misinterpreted. I was equally determined not to appeal to the country at large for funds to conduct this inquiry. For that was likely to give it an all-India and political aspect. Friends from Bombay offered Rs. 15,000, but I declined the offer with thanks. I decided to get as much as was possible, with Brajkishorebabu's help, from well-to-do Biharis living outside Champaran and, if more was needed, to approach my friend Dr. P. J. Mehta of Rangoon. Dr. Mehta readily agreed to send me whatever might be needed. We were thus free from all anxiety on this score. We were not likely to require large funds, as we were bent on exercising the greatest economy in consonance with the poverty of Champaran. Indeed it was found in the end that we did not need any large amount. I have an impression that we expended in all not more than three thousand rupees, and, as far as I remember, we saved a few hundred rupees from what we had collected.

The curious ways of living of my companions in the early days were a constant theme of raillery at their expense. Each of the vakils had a servant and a cook, and therefore a separate kitchen, and they often had their dinner as late as midnight. Though they paid their own expenses, their irregularity worried me, but as we had become close friends there was no possibility of a misunderstanding between us, and they received my ridicule in good part. Ultimately it was agreed that the servants should be dispensed with, that all the kitchens should be amalgamated, and that regular hours should be observed. As all were not vegetarians, and as two kitchens would have been expensive, a common vegetarian kitchen was decided upon. It was also felt necessary to insist on simple meals.

These arrangements considerably reduced the expenses and saved us a lot of time and energy, and both these were badly needed. Crowds of peasants came to make their statements, and they were followed by an army of companions who filled the compound and garden to overflowing. The efforts of my companions to save me from *darshan*-seekers were often of no avail, and I had to be exhibited for *darshan* at particular hours.[9] At least five to seven volunteers were required to take down statements, and even then some people had to go away in the evening without being able to make their statements. All these statements were not essential, many of them being repetitions, but the people could not be satisfied otherwise, and I appreciated their feeling in the matter.

Those who took down the statements had to observe certain rules. Each peasant had to be closely cross-examined, and whoever failed to satisfy the test was rejected. This entailed a lot of extra time but most of the statements were thus rendered incontrovertible.

An officer from the C. I. D. would always be present when these statements were recorded.[10] We might have prevented him, but we had decided from the very beginning not only not to mind the presence of C. I. D. officers, but to treat them with courtesy and to give them all the information that it was possible to give them. This was far from doing us any harm. On the contrary the very fact that the statements were taken down in the presence of the C. I. D. officers made the peasants more fearless. Whilst on the one hand excessive fear of the C. I. D. was driven out of the peasants' minds, on the other, their presence exercised a natural restraint on exaggeration. It was the business of C. I. D. friends to entrap people and so the peasants had necessarily to be cautious.

As I did not want to irritate the planters, but to win them over by gentleness, I made a point of writing to and meeting such of them against whom allegations of a serious nature were made. I met the Planters' Association as well, placed the ryots' grievances before them and acquainted myself with their point of view. Some of the planters hated me, some were indifferent, and a few treated me with courtesy.

As I gained more experience of Bihar, I became convinced that work of a permanent nature was impossible without proper village education. The ryots' ignorance was pathetic. They either allowed their children to roam about, or made them toil on indigo plantations from morning to night for a couple of coppers a day. In those days a male labourer's wage did not exceed ten pice, a female's did not exceed six, and a child's three. He who succeeded in earning four annas a day was considered most fortunate.

In consultation with my companions I decided to open primary schools in six villages. One of our conditions with the villagers was that they should provide the teachers with board and lodging while we would see to the other expenses. The village folk had hardly any cash in their hands, but they could well afford to provide foodstuffs. Indeed they had already expressed their readiness to contribute grain and other raw materials.

From where to get the teachers was a great problem. It was difficult to find local teachers who would work for a bare allowance or without remuneration. My idea was never to entrust children to commonplace teachers. Their literary qualification was not so essential as their moral fibre. So I issued a public appeal for voluntary teachers.

I explained to them that they were expected to teach the children not grammar and the three R's so much as cleanliness and good manners. I further explained that even as regards letters there was not so great a difference between Gujarati, Hindi and Marathi as they imagined, and in the primary classes, at any rate, the teaching of the rudiments of the alphabet and numerals was not a difficult matter. The result was that the classes taken by these ladies were found to be most successful. The experience inspired them with confidence and interest in their work. Avantikabai's became a model school. She threw herself heart and soul into her work. She brought her exceptional gifts to bear on it. Through these ladies we could, to some extent, reach the village women.

But I did not want to stop at providing for primary education. The villages were insanitary, the lanes full of filth, the wells surrounded by mud and stink and the courtyards unbearably untidy. The elder people badly needed education in cleanliness. They were all suffering from various skin diseases. So it was decided to do as much sanitary work as possible and to penetrate every department of their lives.

Doctors were needed for this work. I requested the Servants of India Society to lend us the services of the late Dr. Dev. We had been great friends, and he readily offered his services for six months. The teachers—men and women—had all to work under him.

All of them had express instructions not to concern themselves with grievances against planters or with politics. People who had any complaints to make were to be referred to me. No one was to venture out of his beat. The friends carried out these instructions with wonderful fidelity. I do not remember a single occasion of indiscipline.

As far as was possible we placed each school in charge of one man and one woman. These volunteers had to look after medical relief and sanitation. The womenfolk had to be approached through women.

Medical relief was a very simple affair. Castor oil, quinine and sulphur ointment were the only drugs provided to the volunteers. If the patient showed a furred tongue or complained of constipation, castor oil was administered, in case of fever quinine was given after an opening dose of castor oil, and the sulphur ointment was applied in case of boils and itch after thoroughly washing the affected parts. No patient was permitted to take home any medicine. Wherever there was some complication Dr. Dev. was consulted. Dr. Dev used to visit each centre on certain fixed days in the week.

Quite a number of people availed themselves of this simple relief. This plan of work will not seem strange when it is remembered that the prevailing ailments were few and amenable to simple treatment, by no means requiring expert help. As for the people the arrangement answered excellently.

Sanitation was a difficult affair. The people were not prepared to do anything themselves. Even the field labourers were not ready to do their own scavenging. But Dr. Dev was not a man easily to lose heart. He and the volunteers concentrated their energies on making a village ideally clean. They swept the roads and the courtyards, cleaned out the wells, filled up the pools near by, and lovingly persuaded the villagers to raise volunteers from amongst themselves. In some villages they shamed people into taking up the work, and in others the people were so enthusiastic that they even prepared roads to enable my car to go from place to place. These sweet experiences were not unmixed with bitter ones of people's apathy. I remember some villagers frankly expressing their dislike for this work.

It may not be out of place here to narrate an experience that I have described before now at many meetings. Bhitiharva was a small village in which was one of our schools. I happened to visit a smaller village in its vicinity and found some of the women dressed very dirtily. So I told my wife to ask them why they did not wash their clothes. She spoke to them. One of the women took her into her hut and said: "Look now, there is no box or cupboard here containing other clothes. The sari I am wearing is the only one I have. How am I to wash it? Tell Mahatmaji to get me another sari, and I shall then promise to bathe and put on clean clothes every day."

This cottage was not an exception, but a type to be found in many Indian villages. In countless cottages in India people live without any furniture, and without a change of clothes, merely with a rag to cover their shame.

One more experience I will note. In Champaran

there is no lack of bamboo and grass. The school
hut they had put up at Bhitiharva was made of these
materials. Someone—possibly some of the neighbour-
ing planters' men—set fire to it one night. It was not
thought advisable to build another hut of bamboo and
grass. The school was in charge of Sjt. Soman and
Kasturbai. Sjt. Soman decided to build a *pukka*
house, and thanks to his infectious labour, many
cooperated with him, and a brick house was soon
made ready. There was no fear now of this building
being burnt down.

Thus the volunteers with their schools, sanitation
work and medical relief gained the confidence and
respect of the village folk, and were able to bring
good influence to bear upon them.

But I must confess with regret that my hope of
putting this constructive work on a permanent foot-
ing was not fulfilled. The volunteers had come for
temporary periods, I could not secure any more from
outside, and permanent honorary workers from
Bihar were not available. As soon as my work in
Champaran was finished, work outside, which had
been preparing in the meantime, drew me away. The
few months' work in Champaran, however, took such
deep root that its influence in one form or another
is to be observed there even today.

Whilst on the one hand social service work of the
kind I have described was being carried out, on the
other the work of recording statements of the ryots'
grievances was progressing apace. Thousands of such
statements were taken, and they could not but have

their effect. The ever growing number of ryots coming to make their statements increased the planters'
wrath, and they moved heaven and earth to counter-
act my inquiry.

One day I received a letter from the Bihar Government to the following effect: "Your inquiry has been
sufficiently prolonged; should you not now bring it
to an end and leave Bihar?" The letter was couched in
polite language, but its meaning was obvious.

I wrote in reply that the inquiry was bound to be
prolonged, and unless and until it resulted in bringing relief to the people, I had no intention of leaving
Bihar. I pointed out that it was open to Government
to terminate my inquiry by accepting the ryots'
grievances as genuine and redressing them, or by
recognizing that the ryots had made out a *prima
facie* case for an official inquiry which should be
immediately instituted.

Sir Edward Gait, the Lieutenant Governor, asked
me to see him, expressed his willingness to appoint an
inquiry and invited me to be a member of the Committee. I ascertained the names of the other members,
and after consultation with my co-workers agreed to
serve on the Committee, on condition that I should
be free to confer with my co-workers during the
progress of the inquiry, that Government should
recognize that, by being a member of the Committee,
I did not cease to be the ryots' advocate, and that in
case the result of the inquiry failed to give me satisfaction, I should be free to guide and advise the
ryots as to what line of action they should take.

Sir Edward Gait accepted the condition as just and

proper and announced the inquiry. The late Sir Frank Sly was appointed Chairman of the Committee.

The Committee found in favour of the ryots, and recommend that the planters should refund a portion of the exactions made by them which the Committee had found to be unlawful, and that the *tinkathia* system should be abolished by law.

Sir Edward Gait had a large share in getting the Committee to make a unanimous report and in getting the agrarian bill passed in accordance with the Committee's recommendations. Had he not adopted a firm attitude, and had he not brought all his tact to bear on the subject, the report would not have been unanimous, and the Agrarian Act would not have been passed. The planters wielded extraordinary power. They offered strenuous opposition to the bill in spite of the report, but Sir Edward Gait remained firm up to the last and fully carried out the recommendations of the Committee.

The *tinkathia* system which had been in existence for about a century was thus abolished, and with it the planters' *raj* came to an end.[11] The ryots, who had all along remained crushed, now somewhat came to their own, and the superstition that the stain of indigo could never be washed out was exploded.

It was my desire to continue the constructive work for some years, to establish more schools and to penetrate the villages more effectively. The ground had been prepared, but it did not please God, as often before, to allow my plans to be fulfilled. Fate decided otherwise and drove me to take up work elsewhere.

IX
JAWAHARLAL NEHRU

Clear in thought and in language, extreme in opinion,
determined in action, reckless of consequence, it has
been the lot of Mr. Jawaharlal, who might have
lived a life of ease and luxury, actually to lead a
life of hardship in the service of the Motherland.

C. Y. CHINTAMANI

Introduction

F EW PERSONS have embodied so strikingly the
crisis in modern Indian thought as the undisputed
leader of post-independence India, Jawaharlal Nehru
(1889–   ). His entire career is a testimony to the
complexity of the revolutionary problem and in itself
illustrates each facet of the multiple pattern of conflict in India.

The descendant of a Kashmiri Brahman family, he
was introduced to the issue of reformist Hinduism at

the age of ten, when his father, Motilal, refused to perform the orthodox purification ceremony on his return from England. At thirteen, Nehru joined the eclectic Theosophical Society and was initiated by the ardent Nationalist reformer, Annie Besant. Although he soon lost touch with and sympathy for the Theosophical movement, the experience left a "deep impress" on him.[1] At least it brought him into close contact with the ferment of Hindu theory and reform of that day. As head of an independent India he had later, in a more practical way, to deal with the same issues.

His knowledge of Nationalism and anti-British feeling had even earlier beginnings, during his childhood in Allahabad. He tells of the grown-up talk of his many cousins and their friends, to which he listened avidly in the family home: the resentment against the overbearing manners of the English, the unfair treatment of Indians on the railways and in public places, the bias of English juries. He tells of the beginnings of his own resentment against the presence of "alien rulers," despite his liking for individual Englishmen.[2] In support of his feelings, he was destined to spend much of his adult life in English jails.

His father, Motilal Nehru, had been an admirer of British ways and character, but at the comparatively late age of fifty-six he abandoned his earlier moderate views and became an enthusiastic supporter of the Indian National Congress and the acknowledged Nationalist leader in the United Provinces. His intellectual brilliance, wealth, and prestige gave him tremendous influence in the inner councils of the Congress, in the decade before his death in 1931, a period which saw his imprisonment for anti-Government activity.[3]

When Jawaharlal returned from his studies at Cambridge and his subsequent success at the Bar examinations, he attended the Bankipore Congress meeting of 1912. His father had entered public life five years earlier as president of the United Provinces Conference, and now the son, at the age of twenty-two, was an official Congress delegate. At Bankipore he met the great Gokhale, fresh from South Africa who was "the outstanding person of the session." The young Nehru was impressed: "High-strung, full of earnestness and nervous energy, he seemed to be one of the few persons present who took politics and public affairs seriously and felt deeply about them." [4] He took a keen interest in Gokhale's group, called the Servants of India Society, but because its politics were too moderate and he was not yet ready to abandon the legal profession he did not join that organization. However, he did join the Congress and took part in meetings and occasional agitations.

It was after the coming of Gandhi that an incident shocked him into active anti-British feeling and brought him into intimate contact with "The Mahatma." This event was the Amritsar "massacre" that took place in 1919, and Nehru describes the incident as follows:[5] "Toward the end of that year . . . I traveled to Amritsar by the night train. The compartment I entered was almost full, and all the berths, except one upper one, were occupied by sleeping passengers. I took the vacant upper berth. In the morning I discovered that all my fellow passengers were military officers. They conversed with each other in loud voices which I could not help overhearing. One of them was holding forth in an aggressive and triumphant tone, and soon I discovered that he was Dyer, the hero of Jallianwala Bagh, who was describing his Amritsar experiences. He pointed out how he had the whole town at his mercy and he had felt like reducing the rebellious city to a heap of ashes, but he took pity on it and refrained. He was evidently coming back from Lahore after giving his evidence before the Hunter Committee of Inquiry. I was greatly shocked to hear his conversation and to observe his callous manner. He descended at Delhi station in pyjamas with bright pink stripes, and a dressing gown."

Nehru's attitude toward the Hindu-Moslem communal struggles had been uncompromisingly liberal.[6] His family background in Kashmir and at the Mogul Court led naturally to a high estimate of Moslem civilization, which he refused to consider separate from that of India: "I have tried hard to understand what this 'Moslem Culture' is, but I confess that I have not succeeded. The Moslem peasantry and industrial workers are hardly distinguishable from the Hindu." [7] This outlook was later demonstrated by his refusal to consider the Kashmir problem in terms of racial or cultural issues, as Pakistan did.

He showed great courage and determination in support of the Satyagraha program of Nonviolence, even though he was frank to confess to Gandhi his own reservations concerning it: "For myself I delight in warfare. It makes me feel that I am alive. Events of the last four months in India have gladdened my heart and have made me prouder of Indian men, women, and even children than I have ever been, but I realize that most people are not warlike and like peace and so I try hard to suppress myself and take a peaceful view. May I congratulate you on the new India you have created by your magic touch! . . ." [8] Since India gained her independence, however, Nehru has repeatedly expressed his conviction that the use of violence for obtaining political and social objectives tends to breed more violence, rather than to permanently secure desired ends.

Nehru's early attitude toward Marxian socialism was favorable. "I had long been drawn to socialism and communism, and Russia had appealed to me. Much in Soviet Russia I dislike—the ruthless suppression of all contrary opinion, the wholesale regimentation, the unnecessary violence (as I thought) in carrying out various policies. But there was no lack of violence and suppression in the capitalist world, and I realized more and more how the very basis and foundation of our acquisitive society and property was violence . . . Russia apart, the theory and philosophy of Marxism lightened up many a dark corner of my mind. History came to have a new meaning for me." [9]

The above words were written from a British prison, in 1935. The violence attributed to India's domestic communists, immediately after the war and the partition against railroads and public utilities, the terrorism in Hyderabad—all at a period when India was fighting starvation and anarchy—turned Nehru against the Communist Party and he used counter measures vigorously. At the same time, he maintained cordial relations with foreign communism and assumed a "neutralist" role among the great powers. He has remained deeply dedicated to basic socialist principles, but he has shown increasing coolness toward organized Marxism in India.

After the death of his father, Nehru became the recognized leader of the Congress Party and has remained so ever since, second only to Gandhi in national prestige. The passage which follows is an incident from his campaign experiences which demonstrates some of the forces at work in the shaping of his outlook.

Satyagraha

BY JAWAHARLAL NEHRU

I was returning from Europe in good physical and mental condition.[10] My wife had not yet wholly recovered, but she was far better, and that relieved me of anxiety on her score. I felt full of energy and vitality, and the sense of inner conflict and frustration that had oppressed me so often previously was, for the time being, absent. My outlook was wider, and nationalism by itself seemed to me definitely a narrow and insufficient creed. Political freedom, independence, were no doubt essential, but they were steps only in the right direction; without social freedom and a socialistic structure of society and the State, neither the country nor the individual could develop much. I felt I had a clearer perception of world affairs, more grip on the present-day world, ever changing as it was. I had read largely, not only on current affairs and politics, but on many other subjects that interested me, cultural and scientific. I found the vast political, economic, and cultural changes going on in Europe and America a fascinating study. Soviet Russia, despite certain unpleasant aspects, attracted me greatly, and seemed to hold forth a message of hope to the world. Europe, in the middle twenties, was trying to settle down in a way; the great depression was yet to come. But I came back with the conviction that this settling down was superficial only, and big eruptions and mighty changes were in store for Europe and the world in the near future.

To train and prepare our country for these world events—to keep in readiness for them, as far as we could—seemed to be the immediate task. The preparation was largely an ideological one. First of all, there should be no doubt about the objective of political independence. This should be clearly understood as the only possible political goal for us; something radically different from the vague and confusing talk of Dominion status. Then there was the social goal. It would be too much, I felt, to expect the Congress to go far in this direction just then. The Congress was a purely political and nationalistic body, unused to thinking on other lines. But a beginning might be made. Outside the Congress, in labor circles and among the young, the idea could be pushed on much further. For this purpose I wanted to keep myself free from Congress office, and I had a vague idea also of spending some months in remote rural areas to study their conditions. But this was not to be, and events were to drag me again into the heart of Congress politics.

Immediately on our arrival in Madras I was caught in the whirl. I presented a bunch of resolutions to the Working Committee—resolutions on independence, war danger, association with the League against Imperialism, etc.—and nearly all of these were accepted and made into official Working Committee resolutions. I had to put them forward at the open session of the Congress, and, to my surprise, they were all almost unanimously adopted. The Independence resolution was supported even by Mrs. Annie Besant. This all-round support was very gratifying, but I had an uncomfortable feeling that the resolutions were either not understood for what they were, or were distorted to mean something else. That this was so became apparent soon after the Congress, when a controversy arose on the meaning of the Independence resolution.

These resolutions of mine were somewhat different from the usual Congress resolutions; they represented a new outlook. Many Congressmen no doubt liked them, some had a vague dislike for them, but not enough to make them oppose. Probably the latter thought that they were academic resolutions, making little difference either way, and the best way to get rid of them was to pass them and move on to something more important. The Independence resolution thus did not represent then, as it did a year or two later, a vital and irrepressible urge on the part of the Congress; it represented a widespread and growing sentiment.

Gandhiji was in Madras, and he attended the open Congress sessions, but he did not take any part in the shaping of policy. He did not attend the meetings of the Working Committee, of which he was a member. That had been his general political attitude in the Congress since the dominance of the Swaraj party. But he was frequently consulted, and little of importance was done without his knowledge. I do not know how far the resolutions I put before the Congress met with his approval. I am inclined to think that he disliked them, not so much because of what they said, but because of their general trend and outlook. He did not, however, criticize them on any occasion.

The unreality of the Independence resolution came out in that very session of the Congress, when another resolution condemning the Simon Commission and appealing for its boycott was considered.[11] As a corollary to this it was proposed to convene an All-Parties Conference, which was to draw up a constitution for India. It was manifest that the moderate groups, with whom co-operation was sought, could never think in terms of independence. The very utmost they could go to was some form of Dominion status.

I stepped back into the Congress secretaryship. There were personal considerations—the desire of the president for the year, Dr. M. A. Ansari, who was an old and dear friend—and the fact that, as many of my resolutions had been passed, I ought to see them through. It was true that the resolution on the All-Parties Conference had partly neutralized the effect of my resolutions. Still, much remained. The real reason for my accepting office again was my fear that the Congress might, through the instrumentality of the All-Parties Conference, or because of other reasons, slide back to a more moderate and compromising position. It seemed to be in a hesitant mood, swinging alternately from one extreme to another. I wanted to prevent, as far as I could, the swing back to moderation and to hold on to the independence objective.

The National Congress always attracts a large number of side shows at its annual sessions. One of the side shows at Madras was a Republican Conference which held its first (and last) sessions that year. I was asked to preside. The idea appealed to me, as I considered myself a republican. But I hesitated, as I did not know who was at the back of the new venture, and I did not want to associate myself with mushroom growths. I presided, eventually, but later I repented of this, for the Republican Conference turned out to be, like so many others, a still-born affair. For several months I tried, and tried in vain, to get the text of the resolutions passed by it. It is amazing how many of our people love to sponsor new undertakings and then ignore them and leave them to shift for themselves. There is much in the criticism that we are not a persevering lot.

I have been accused by some leaders of the Hindu Mahasabha of my ignorance of Hindu sentiments because of my defective education and general background of "Persian" culture.[12] What culture I possess, or whether I possess any at all, is a little difficult for me to say. Persian, as a language, unhappily, I do not even know. But it is true that my father had grown up in an Indo-Persian cultural atmosphere, which was the legacy in north India of the old Delhi court, and of which, even in these degenerate days, Delhi and Lucknow are the two chief centers. Kashmiri Brahmans had a remarkable capacity for adaptation, and coming down to the Indian plains and finding that this Indo-Persian culture was predominant at the time, they took to it, and produced a number of fine scholars in Persian and Urdu. Later they adapted themselves with equal rapidity to the changing order, when a knowledge of English and the elements of European culture became necessary.

The year 1928 was, politically, a full year, with plenty of activity all over the country. There seemed to be a new impulse moving the people forward, a new stir that was equally present in the most varied groups. Probably the change had been going on gradually during my long absence from the country; it struck me as very considerable on my return. Early in 1926, India was still quiescent, passive, perhaps not fully recovered from the effort of 1919–1922;[13] in 1928 she seemed fresh, active, and full of suppressed energy. Everywhere there was evidence of this: among the industrial workers, the peasantry, middle-class youth, and the intelligentsia generally. The trade-union movement had grown greatly, and the All-India Trade-Union Congress, established seven or eight years previously, was already a strong and representative body. The peasantry was also astir. This was noticeable in the United Provinces and especially in Oudh, where large gatherings of protesting tenants became common. Another very noticeable feature of the India of 1928 was the growth of the youth movement. Everywhere youth leagues were being established, youth conferences were being held.

Wherever the Commission went it was greeted by hostile crowds and the cry of "Simon, go back," and thus vast numbers of the Indian masses became acquainted not only with Sir John Simon's name but with two words of the English language, the only two they knew. These words must have become a hated obsession for the members of the Commission. The story is related that once, when they were staying at the Western Hostel in New Delhi, the refrain seemed to come to them in the night out of the darkness. They were greatly irritated at being pursued in this way, even at night. As a matter of fact, the noise that disturbed them came from the jackals that infest the waste places of the imperial capital.

The All-Parties Conference met at Lucknow to consider the report of their committee. Again some of us were in a dilemma, for we did not wish to come in

the way of a communal settlement, if that was possible, and yet we were not prepared to yield on the
question of independence. We begged that the conference leave this question open so that each consti-
tuent part could have liberty of action on this issue
—the Congress adhering to independence and the
more moderate groups to Dominion status. But my
father had set his heart on the report, and he would
not yield, nor perhaps could he under the circumstances. I was thereupon asked by our independence
group in the Conference—and this was a large one
—to make a statement to the Conference on its behalf,
dissociating ourselves completely from everything that
lowered the objective of independence. But we made
it further clear that we would not be obstructive as we
did not wish to come in the way of the communal
statement.

This was not a very effective line to adopt on such a
major issue; at best it was a negative gesture. A positive
side was given to our attitude by our founding that
very day the Independence for India League.

The Simon Commission was moving about, pursued
by black flags and hostile crowds shouting, "Go back."
Occasionally there were minor conflicts between the
police and the crowds. Lahore brought matters to a
head and suddenly sent a thrill of indignation throughout the country. The anti-Simon Commission demonstration there was headed by Lala Lajpat Rai; and,
as he stood by the roadside in front of the thousands
of demonstrators, he was assaulted and beaten on his
chest with a baton by a young English police officer.
There had been no attempt whatever on the part of

the crowd, much less on the part of Lalaji, to indulge
in any methods of violence. Even so, as he stood
peacefully by, he and many of his companions were
severely beaten by the police. Anyone who takes part
in street demonstrations runs the risk of a conflict with
the police, and, though our demonstrations were
almost always perfectly peaceful, Lalaji must have
known of this risk and taken it consciously. But still,
the manner of the assault, the needless brutality of
it, came as a shock to vast numbers of people in
India. Those were the days when we were not used to
lathee charges by the police; our sensitiveness had
not been blunted by repeated brutality. To find that
even the greatest of our leaders, the foremost and
most popular man in the Punjab, could be so treated
seemed little short of monstrous, and a dull anger
spread all over the country, especially in north India.
How helpless we were, how despicable when we could
not even protect the honor of our chosen leaders!

The physical injury to Lalaji had been serious
enough, as he had been hit on the chest and he had
long suffered from heart disease. Probably, in the case
of a healthy young man the injury would not have
been great, but Lalaji was neither young nor healthy.
What effect this physical injury had on his death a
few weeks later it is hardly possible to say definitely,
though his doctors were of opinion that it hastened
the end. But I think that there can be no doubt that
the mental shock which accompanied the physical
injury had a tremendous effect on Lalaji. He felt
angry and bitter, not so much at the personal humilia-

tion, as at the national humiliation involved in the assault on him.

It was this sense of national humiliation that weighed on the mind of India, and when Lalaji's death came soon after, inevitably it was connected with the assault, and sorrow itself gave pride of place to anger and indignation. It is well to appreciate this, for only so can we have some understanding of subsequent events, of the phenomenon of Bhagat Singh, and of his sudden and amazing popularity in north India.[14] It is very easy and very fatuous to condemn persons or acts without seeking to understand the springs of action, the causes that underlie them. Bhagat Singh was not previously well known; he did not become popular because of an act of violence, an act of terrorism. Terrorists have flourished in India, off and on, for nearly thirty years, and at no time, except in the early days in Bengal, did any of them attain a fraction of that popularity which came to Bhagat Singh. This is a patent fact which cannot be denied; it has to be admitted. And another fact, which is equally obvious, is that terrorism, in spite of occasional recrudescence, has no longer any real appeal for the youth of India. Fifteen years' stress on nonviolence has changed the whole background in India and made the masses much more indifferent to, and even hostile to, the idea of terrorism as a method of political action. Even the classes from which the terrorists are usually drawn, the lower middle-classes and intelligentsia, have been powerfully affected by the Congress propaganda against methods of violence.

Their active and impatient elements, who think in terms of revolutionary action, also realize fully now that revolution does not come through terrorism, and that terrorism is an outworn and profitless method which comes in the way of real revolutionary action. Terrorism is a dying thing in India and elsewhere, not because of Government coercion, which can only suppress and bottle up, not eradicate, but because of basic causes and world events. Terrorism usually represents the infancy of a revolutionary urge in a country. That stage passes, and with it passes terrorism as an important phenomenon. Occasional outbursts may continue because of local causes or individual suppressions. India has undoubtedly passed that stage, and no doubt even the occasional outbursts will gradually die out. But this does not mean that all people in India have ceased to believe in methods of violence. They have, very largely, ceased to believe in individual violence and terrorism, but many, no doubt, still think that a time may come when organized, violent methods may be necessary for gaining freedom, as they have often been necessary in other countries. That is today an academic issue which time alone will put to the test; it has nothing to do with terroristic methods.

Bhagat Singh thus did not become popular because of his act of terrorism, but because he seemed to vindicate, for the moment, the honor of Lala Lajpat Rai, and through him of the nation. He became a symbol; the act was forgotten, the symbol remained, and within a few months each town and village of the Punjab, and to a lesser extent in the rest of northern

India, resounded with his name. Innumerable songs grew up about him, and the popularity that the man achieved was something amazing.

The assault on Lala Lajpat Rai, and his subsequent death, increased the vigor of the demonstrations against the Simon Commission in the places which it subsequently visited. It was due in Lucknow, and the local Congress committee made extensive preparations for its "reception." Huge processions, meetings, and demonstrations were organized many days in advance, both as propaganda and as rehearsals for the actual show. I went to Lucknow and was present at some of these. The success of these preliminary demonstrations, which were perfectly orderly and peaceful, evidently nettled the authorities, and they began to obstruct and issue orders against the taking out of processions in certain areas. It was in this connection that I had a new experience, and my body felt the baton and lathee blows of the police.

Processions had been prohibited, ostensibly to avoid any interference with the traffic. We decided to give no cause for complaint on this score, and arranged for small groups of sixteen, as far as I can remember, to go separately, along unfrequented routes to the meeting place. Technically, this was no doubt a breach of the order, for sixteen with a flag were a procession. I led one of the groups of sixteen and, after a big gap, came another such group under the leadership of my colleague, Govind Ballabh Pant.[15] My group had gone perhaps about two hundred yards—the road was a deserted one—when we heard the clatter of horses' hoofs behind us. We looked back to find a

bunch of mounted police, probably two or three
dozen in number, bearing down upon us at a rapid
pace. They were soon right upon us, and the impact
of the horses broke up our little column of sixteen.
The mounted policemen then started belaboring our
volunteers with huge batons or truncheons, and,
instinctively, the volunteers sought refuge on the side-
walks, and some even entered the petty shops. They
were pursued and beaten down. My own instinct had
urged me to seek safety when I saw the horses charging
down upon us; it was a discouraging sight. But then,
I suppose, some other instinct held me to my place,
and I survived the first charge, which had been checked
by the volunteers behind me. Suddenly I found myself alone in the middle of the road; a few yards away
from me, in various directions, were the policemen
beating down our volunteers. Automatically, I began
moving slowly to the side of the road to be less
conspicuous, but again I stopped and had a little
argument with myself, and decided that it would be
unbecoming for me to move away. All this was a
matter of a few seconds only, but I have the clearest
recollections of that conflict within me and the decision, prompted by my pride, I suppose, which could
not tolerate the idea of my behaving like a coward.
Yet the line between cowardice and courage was a
thin one, and I might well have been on the other
side. Hardly had I so decided, when I looked round to
find that a mounted policeman was trotting up to
me, brandishing his long new baton. I told him to go
ahead, and turned my head away—again an instinc-
tive effort to save the head and face. He gave me two

resounding blows on the back. I felt stunned, and my body quivered all over, but, to my surprise and satisfaction, I found that I was still standing. The police force was withdrawn soon after and made to block the road in front of us. Our volunteers gathered together again, many of them bleeding and with split skulls, and we were joined by Pant and his lot, who had also been belabored, and all of us sat down facing the police. So we sat for an hour or so, and it became dark. On the one side, various high officials gathered; on the other, large crowds began to assemble as the news spread. Ultimately, the officials agreed to allow us to go by our original route, and we went that way with the mounted policemen, who had charged us and belabored us, going ahead of us as a kind of escort.

I have written about this petty incident in some detail because of its effect on me. The bodily pain I felt was quite forgotten in a feeling of exhilaration that I was physically strong enough to face and bear lathee blows. And a thing that surprised me was that right through the incident, even when I was being beaten, my mind was quite clear and I was consciously analyzing my feelings. This rehearsal stood me in good stead the next morning, when a stiffer trial was in store for us. For the next morning was the time when the Simon Commission was due to arrive, and our great demonstration was going to take place. My father was at Allahabad at the time, and I was afraid that the news of the assault on me, when he read about it in the next morning's papers, would upset him and the rest of the family. So I telephoned to him late in the evening to assure him that all was well and that he should not worry. But he did worry, and, finding it difficult to sleep over it, he decided at about midnight to come over to Lucknow. The last train had gone, and so he started by motor-car. He had some bad luck on the way, and it was nearly five in the morning by the time he had covered the journey of 146 miles and reached Lucknow, tired out and exhausted.

That was about the time when we were getting ready to go in procession to the station. The previous evening's incidents had the effect of rousing up Lucknow more than anything that we could have done, and, even before the sun was out, vast numbers of people made their way to the station. Innumerable little processions came from various parts of the city, and from the Congress office started the main procession, consisting of several thousands, marching in fours. we were in this main procession. We were stopped by the police as we approached the station. There was a huge open space, about half a mile square, in front of the station (this has now been built over by the new station) and we were made to line up on one side of this Maidan, and there our procession remained, making no attempt to push our way forward. The place was full of foot and mounted police, as well as the military. The crowd of sympathetic onlookers swelled up, and many of these persons managed to spread out in twos and threes in the open space. Suddenly we saw in the far distance a moving mass. It was two or three long lines of cavalry or mounted police, covering the entire area, galloping down toward us, and striking and riding down the numerous stragglers that dotted the Maidan. That charge of galloping horsemen was a fine sight, but for the tragedies that were being enacted on the way, as harmless and very much surprised sight-seers went under the horses' hoofs. Behind the charging lines these people lay on the ground, some still unable to move, others writhing in pain, and the whole appearance of that Maidan was that of a battlefield. But we did not have much time for gazing on that scene or for reflections; the horsemen were soon upon us, and their front line clashed almost at a gallop with the massed ranks of our processionists. We held our ground, and, as we appeared to be unyielding, the horses had to pull up at the last moment and reared up on their hind legs with their front hoofs quivering in the air over our heads. And then began a beating of us, and battering with lathees and long batons both by the mounted and the foot police. It was a tremendous hammering, and the clearness of vision that I had had the evening before left me. All I knew was that I had to stay where I was and must not yield or go back. I felt half blinded with the blows, and sometimes a dull anger seized me and a desire to hit out. I thought how easy it would be to pull down the police officer in front of me from his horse and to mount up myself, but long training and discipline held, and I did not raise a hand, except to protect my face from a blow. Besides, I knew well enough that any aggression on our part would result in a ghastly tragedy, the shooting down of large numbers of our men.

After what seemed a tremendous length of time, but was probably only a few minutes, our line began

149

to yield slowly, step by step, without breaking up. This left me somewhat isolated, and more exposed at the sides. More blows came, and then I was suddenly lifted off my feet from behind and carried off, to my great annoyance. Some of my younger colleagues, thinking that a dead set was being made at me, had decided to protect me in this summary fashion.

Our processionists lined up again about a hundred feet behind our original line. The police also withdrew and stood in a line, fifty feet apart from us. So we remained, when the cause of all this trouble, the Simon Commission, secretly crept away from the station in the far distance, more than a half a mile away. But, even so, they did not escape the back flags or demonstrators. Soon after, we came back in full procession to the Congress office and there dispersed, and I went on to [my] father, who was anxiously waiting for us.

Now that the excitement of the moment had passed, I felt pains all over my body and great fatigue. Almost every part of me seemed to ache, and I was covered with contused wounds and marks of blows. But fortunately I was not injured in any vital spot. Many of our companions were less fortunate, and were badly injured. Govind Ballabh Pant, who stood by me, offered a much bigger target, being six foot odd in height, and the injuries he received then have resulted in a painful and persistent malady which prevented him for a long time from straightening his back or leading an active life. I emerged with a somewhat greater conceit of my physical condition and powers of endurance. But the memory that endures

with me, far more than that of the beating itself, is
that of many of the faces of those policemen, and
especially of the officers, who were attacking us. Most
of the real beating and battering was done by European sergeants; the Indian rank and file were milder
in their methods. And those faces, full of hate and
blood-lust, almost mad, with no trace of sympathy or
touch of humanity! Probably the faces on our side
just then were equally hateful to look at, and the fact
that we were mostly passive did not fill our minds and
hearts with love for our opponents, or add to the
beauty of our countenances. And yet, we had no griev-
ance against each other; no quarrel that was personal,
no ill will. We happened to represent, for the time
being, strange and thither, and, subtly gripping our
minds and hearts, roused our desires and passions and
made us their blind tools. Blindly we struggled, not
knowing what we struggled for and whither we went.
The excitement of action held us; but, as it passed,
immediately the question arose: To what end was all
this? To what end?

X
SARVEPALLI RADHAKRISHNAN

The tradition of the Rishi is alive in India today. Sarvepalli Radhakrishnan is the twentieth century equivalent of the ancient Hindu Rishi. He is a presence felt and known in the councils of the nation.

D. B. DHANAPALA

Introduction

INDIA'S BEST KNOWN PHILOSOPHER entered the political scene rather late in life and only after he had established a brilliant reputation as author and lecturer on Oriental thought and culture. Born near Madras and educated in that city, Sarvepalli Radhakrishnan (1888–   ) taught philosophy there from 1909 to 1917. For the next twenty years he taught at Mysore and Calcutta Universities and was called to lecture at

Oxford, Cambridge, Harvard, Buenos Aires and other institutions. His best known work, the scholarly two-volume treatise entitled *Indian Philosophy*, was completed in 1926. Other publications include: *The Hindu View of Life*; *Kalki, or the Future of Civilization*; *Eastern Religions and Western Thought*; and *Education, Politics and War*. His achievements brought him nomination, in 1931, to the old League of Nations Committee for Intellectual Coöperation. Thereafter, in Western eyes he was the recognized Hindu authority on Indian ideas and a persuasive interpreter of the role of Eastern institutions in contemporary society.

It is therefore not surprising that Dr. Radhakrishnan should have been called to serve in high office in the government of independent India, though his background was not one of service to the Congress Party and strenuous struggle against British rule. He had always defended Hindu culture against uninformed Western criticism and had symbolized the pride of Indians in their own intellectual traditions. He describes how, as a student, "The challenge of Christian critics impelled me to make a study of Hinduism and find out what is living and what is dead in it. My pride as a Hindu, roused by the enterprise and eloquence of Swami Vivekananda, was deeply hurt by the treatment accorded to Hinduism in missionary institutions." [1] After the Second World War he was able, as a member of the Executive Board of UNESCO, to continue the role he had played in the old League of Nations Committee by presenting India's position in international educational and cultural issues.[2] In 1949 he was appointed Ambassador to the Soviet Union, and in 1952 was elected Vice President of India.

The following passages by Rhadhakrishnan reveal how thoroughly he has mastered the intellectual contributions of the West. At the same time, his deep commitment to Indian cultural ideals brings him to offer criticisms and insights to be found only in one dedicated to the traditions of tolerance and nonviolence associated with his Hindu background.

Morality and Politics (1938)

BY SARVEPALLI RADHAKRISHNAN

When I was a student, nearly thirty years ago, we had great faith in the ideals of science and education, democracy and peace—with the growth of science we thought we would conquer pain; with the spread of education and enlightenment, we imagined that we would banish ignorance and superstition; with the extension of democratic institutions we hoped that we would remove all injustice and move towards an earthly paradise: with the increase of humanitarian sentiments we thought wars would be abolished. We believed that we could use intelligence in our dealings with physical environment, our social institutions and our inmost selves—we assumed that it was all a question of technology or engineering like control of floods of improvement of communications.

Science has increased its range and scope, education has spread widely but we are not so sure that life is richer or the future brighter. The failure of the intellectual devices to improve our social relations has brought disappointment to the human soul. We find that the creation of ideal human relations is a different problem from the mastery of nature. The problem of living has become much more complicated and the mood in which we have to face it is not that of the self-complacent intellectual.

If mankind finds itself in a mess, if things which should contribute to humanity's wealth have become an occasion for failing, it is because our conceptions of life are superficial. Human nature is not a matter of surfaces but of strata, of external experience, of reflective consciousness, of moral and aesthetic apprehension, of religious insight. Every stratum has its own life. We have diseases of the body as well as of the mind. If cold and catarrh are illnesses of physical nature, if error, prejudice and falsehood are defects of our mind, lust, anger and jealousy are deformations of our heart. However much we may progress in the conquest of natural forces or in the control of social injustices, a very important part of the human problem will consist in the disciplining of our wayward desires and the achievement of an attitude of poise toward the inevitable limitations of finite existence.

The natural desire of man is to be good and seek the true. No teaching can create this desire out of the void. No truth can be taught unless the potentiality for knowing it is already there in the spirit of the pupil. The instinct of spiritual life is in human nature. Religion is not a mere eccentricity, not an historical accident, not a psychological device, not an escape mechanism, not an economic lubricant induced by an indifferent world. It is an integral element of human nature, an intimation of destiny, a perception of the value of the individual, an awareness of the importance of human choice for the future of the world. It is a cleansing of man's soul, a sense for the mystery of the universe, a feeling of tenderness and compassion for one's fellowmen and the humbler creatures of life. To have religious men as the components of a society makes all the difference in the life of that society.

The world has moved through different periods and we are now in what may be called the first era of world civilization. The invention and spread of new means of rapid communication affecting both the movement of persons and the transfer of ideas have made the world into a single whole. This intermingling of races and cultures makes it possible for the world to grow into a moral community, a single commonwealth in which the human race will find ordered peace, settled government, material prosperity, the reign of law and freedom for all, which is the goal towards which all previous history has been leading. The instinct for such a community is in human nature. The ordinary human being is decent, is peacefully inclined, hates bloodshed, has no joy in battle. This fundamental humanity has kept our race going. It is to be seen in the mother at the cradle of her child, in the ploughman at his furrow, in the scientist in his laboratory and in the young and the old when they love and worship. The love of man, this faith in the moral structure of society has upheld the spirit of man against many tyrannies and shall uphold it still.

Men, as we find them, however, are artificial products. We are made one way and society remakes us in another. Our relationships with fellow-beings have become unnatural and artificial. We are made to feel, not that we are human but that we are Hindu or Moslem, French or German, Jew or Gentile. Our barbarous laws and institutions seduce us from our natural feelings of sympathy and fellowship. Fear, suspicion and resentment arise and wars which become each year more destructive are waged for the glory of the fictional abstractions of race and nation, class and creed. The world cannot permanently organise its life in an unjust and unnatural way without reaping chaos and conflict. The root cause of our present trouble is an interdependent world worked on a particularist basis. If moral principles are set at naught, if we are not faithful to the instinct of the common man, nemesis will overtake us.

We are filled with despair by the violence of the contemporary world. Recent events in China, Abyssinia, Czechoslovakia and Spain constitute a betrayal of moral values.[3] Faith and hope have all but succumbed. Honour and magnanimity have decayed. The hot embers of sullen discontent and savage hatred smoulder everywhere. A peace which arises from mere weariness of war and founded on international injustice and political opportunism has no element of permanence in it. The immense armaments in process of anxious accumulation in Great Britain, France and the United States of America do not give us any feeling of security. The world is shaken and exhausted and man has become an anguished being, living in the uncertainty of tomorrow, left alien in a world where there is neither joy nor love nor light nor certitude nor peace nor help for pain. The world is on fire and the sparks are flying. What is there to cling to in a world of madness and doom, of waste and hideousness? The whole machinery of modern civilisation is failing to perform even the basic function of keeping men alive. A world in agony asks, "Is civilisation to end up in a mangled mass of twisted metal and torn flesh?" This cry of pain is indeed evidence that in spite of its sickness the body is alive and fighting for life. Though we must deeply deplore the outlawry, the savagery, the wantonness of the present, there is hope in that the fallow ground of the whole world is being broken up. Broken soil is full of promise.

It is easy to blame the Germans, the Italians and the Japanese for the present condition of the world, but they are like ourselves. We, perhaps, in their condition will do the same. Their weaknesses and virtues are in profound solidarity with our weaknesses and virtues. The development is the outgrowth of an environment heavily weighted with tragedy and failure, mistakes and misunderstandings, resentments and hatreds. Take, for example, the case of the Germans. They lost a war and an incompetent government slipped in after the fall of the monarchy, while the best part of

the nation was still in the front. They suffered igno-
miny and hardships at the hands of the victors in the
post-war period. They writhed under military invasion
and financial subjection in peace time. To restore
national pride and self-confidence, to resist the threat
of a proletarian philosophy which increased middle
class anxiety, the Nazi movement sprang up. We
would not have behaved differently if we were in the
position of the Germans. The problem ahead of us
is a universal problem, a problem of humanity, not of
this or that country.

The world has seen a number of civilisations on
which the dust of ages has settled. The jungle has
conquered their great centres and jackals howl there
in the moonlight. The spade of the archaeologist
uncovers for us dead cities that we may behold in
them our pride and our shame. We assumed that
whatever may be the changes and developments, the
solid structure of Western Civilisation was itself
enduring and permanent, but we now see how appall-
ingly insecure it is. The menace of war has been a
writing on the wall. The present world situation is a
spiritual challenge. We must either accept it or
perish. It is not safe to be immoral. Evil systems
inevitably destroy themselves by their own greed and
egotism. Against the rock of moral law, earth's conquerors and exploiters hurl themselves eventually to
their own destruction. While yet there is time, there
is not much left, we must take steps to prevent the
helpless rush of man to his doom.

Revolutions rest on basic psychological changes in
the minds of men. A certain degree of soul, Ben

Jonson maintained, is indispensable to keep the body from destruction. If we would save the world from decay, we must do something to it with our spirit. We have to rebuild the city in the soul which has been so disastrously invaded by the false gods of pride and power and undermined by selfishness and stupidity.

A new generation is growing up with a new awareness of the oneness of humanity. It understands that peace is a positive achievement, calling for high enterprise. It is aware that world peace demands world justice and the obstacles to it are in the hearts of men which have been corrupted, in their prides and jealousies, in their attachment to comforts and possessions at other people's expense. National ambitions and racial passions blind us to real ends and long views. Unless we remove the sources of injustice and fear, we cannot make the world safe for peace. The history of man has been a continual struggle between the ideal of a moral community and the immoral forces of greed, stupidity and violence, individual and corporate. We must refine the spirit of patriotism so as to make it a pathway from man to mankind. A world conference to examine territorial grievances, control of raw materials and possibilities of collateral disarmament and establish the freedom of all nations, small or great, weak or strong may be summoned and if the powerful nations approach the task in a chastened spirit and in the faith that nations like individuals are great not by what they acquire but by what they resign, we may get nearer our goal.

Great Britain can work for a liberal and democratic civilisation by transforming her empire into a commonwealth of free nations and that will be her greatest contribution to a better world order. It is difficult to understand her foreign policy or her Indian policy. It is unimaginable how Great Britain and France could view with indifference, if not sympathy, the consolidation of the dictatorships. If the present policy is persisted in, very soon, Holland and Belgium, Switzerland and Scandinavia will get into the orbit of the Berlin-Rome axis. Even today the British Government seems to be genuinely indifferent to the kind of government which will emerge from the Spanish war. No one can say with confidence what Great Britain will do in the matter of the Colonies or German advance into Ukraine. One explanation is that class feeling has prevailed over patriotism among the governing classes of Britain. Another is that the British people have lost their ambition and their ingrained sense of being the greatest power in the world and so have yielded to other powers and themselves suffered a loss of strength and prestige.

In a disordered world we seem to occupy a sheltered position and enjoy in some measure the amenities of civilised life. In the British Empire our position is a junior and subordinate one. So far as our defences go, we are in a helpless condition. Even now a great menace to the peace and safety of our country is growing up in the Far East and its tremors are felt in Siam and Burma. Germany is striving to extend her influence through Asia Minor, Iraq, Iran and Afghanistan to the frontiers of India. In the dangerous condition of the world, where three great powers are

acting in concert, adopting the doctrine of force as
the inspiration of their policies, Britain must reaffirm
her faith in freedom and democracy, not by words but
by deeds and weld together the different dominions
into unity on the basis of devotion to the ideals. Self-
interest, international decency and justice demand
the establishment of self-government in India. The
most urgent problem is to work out a federation, not
on the lines of the Government of India Act, but on
lines which will foster and further internal unity
among the different communities and between provinces and States.[4] So long as India has to submit
to a constitution imposed on her, she is not free. One
of the greatest historians of the world, the German
Theodor Mommsen, emphasises a truth which modern
Germany has forgotten and Great Britain will have
to remember if her methods are to be distinguished
from those of Germany. "According to the same law
of nature in virtue of which the smallest organism
infinitely surpasses the most artistic machine, every
constitution however defective, which gives play to
the free self-determination of a majority of citizens
infinitely surpasses the most brilliant and humane
absolutism, for the former is capable of development
and therefore living; the latter is what it is and therefore dead." [5] If Britain fails to develop in time a
strong and self-governing India, she cannot escape
the destruction which has overcome empires as proud
and seemingly as firmly rooted as her own. No nation
is fully grown up until it has been purged of egotism
and pride.

The Fruits of Victory (1941)

What is the root-cause of war? Why are wars recurrent phenomena in human history? Why do we have the present holocaust of youth, which threatens to engulf the whole world? Why is it that after centuries of enlightenment we are unable to settle our quarrels in a peaceful manner? Why are we fighting? When we try to analyse the causes of the war, we may limit our attention to the immediate causes, or the remote causes or the deeper ones. If we say that Hitler's unprovoked attack on Poland is the cause of the war, we will not be quite accurate. Even as late as 1931 the Government of Britain declined to support the protest of the Government of the United States against Japan's wanton invasion of China.[6] Since then we have had unprovoked attacks on Ethiopia, Austria, Spain, and Czechoslovakia, Lithuania and Albania. If we go back a little, and look for the causes in the Versailles Treaty, the failure of the League of Nations, and the Disarmament Conference, we do not get to the bottom of it all. If the Versailles Treaty was unjust, it was a treaty imposed by the victors on the vanquished. If the League and the Disarmament Conference failed, it is because the spirit

necessary for their success was lacking. The root-causes
of the war lie in the undemocratic structure of our
society, in a kind of tribal patriotism and a passion
for power by which all nations are possessed.

Pericles in his funeral oration makes out that Athens
is the school of Hellas, and called upon the brave
Athenians to die for winning the leadership of Hellas
which he refused to share with Sparta. "We have
compelled" he says, "every sea and every land to
admit our prowess, and everywhere we have planted
memorials of harm to our enemies, of good to our
friends. For such a city these men have nobly fought,
and they have given their lives to prove their faith
in the inviolableness of their city; let every one of you
left alive be willing to suffer as much for Athens." He
goes on: "These men held the chastisement of the
enemy more dear, and preferred the glorious risk of
avenging themselves upon him. And when the hour
of battle was at hand, thinking it a finer thing to
defend themselves and die than to yield and live,
they fled from the word 'dishonour,' but held fast to
the noble deed. These men behaved as befits the city.
You will be wiser to contemplate day by day the might
of your city and become her passionate lovers, letting
her grandeur and her glory inspire you to reflect
that it was all gained by brave men who knew their
duty, by men who, when they failed in any enterprise,
did not bereave the city of their virtue, but gave
freely the fairest commonweal, and thus won for
themselves unfading praise and a most famous tomb
—not that in which lie their bones, but that in which

their glory lives in eternal remembrance to be cele-
brated by every opportunity of word or deed. Of
famous men the whole world is the tomb. Do you
now emulate these men, and counting happiness as
liberty, as courage, do not worry yourselves about the
danger of war."

Do we not hear the echo of these ringing words in
the British Premier's utterances? [7] "We shall never
stop, never weary, never give in, and our whole people
and Empire have vowed themselves to the task of
cleansing Europe from the Nazi pestilence and saving
the world from a new Dark Age; we seek to beat the
life and soul out of Hitler and Hitlerism. That alone,
that all the time, and that to the end." In this tremendous epoch, "England's finest hour," he exhorts
Englishmen to accept "blood, and toil, tears and
sweat." It seems to be the same story, the same problem, the same fight. The play goes on; only the actors
change and the scales alter. Instead of the leadership
of Hellas we have the leadership of the world. Instead
of Athens and Sparta we have the Allied and the
Axis powers. We are fighting for the good old cause of
civilisation and freedom. We are fighting against evil
things, said the late Mr. Neville Chamberlain. It is a
conflict between the good and the evil, between the
graces of civilisation and the rawness of barbarism.
But is it all quite so simple? Why should a great
people like the Germans with their magnificent
record of achievement and influence in every sphere
of intellectual life, literature and philosophy, arts and
sciences become the blind followers of a monstrous

materialism? Again, the forces of civilisation won times without number but we are not better off. The evil is still there.

Why should we labour, plan and found families if the world will continue to be a jungle where nations like beasts of prey are led by a blind instinct to destroy others on pain of being destroyed by them? Why should millions of men be called upon to suffer and die just to enable one of the powers to assume the leadership of the world? Only the greatest of causes, the securing of permanent peace and a world of co-operating nations, can justify the unspeakable agony of our times. If a durable peace and a stable world are to be built out of the wreckage of this war, we must have a positive conception of the values for which we stand. The fate of the human race depends on its moral strength, and moral power consists here as elsewhere in renunciation and self-limitation. A civilised society is possible only in an ordered community where there is a rule of law before which the poor man and the rich, the weak nation and the strong are equal, which believes that the world belongs to all. In this war, the British appeal to the great ideals of democracy and freedom. Democracy means a system of government which gives ultimate power to the ordinary man, which gives freedom within law to believe, write or say what we please, where government is carried on by free discussion, toleration and national adjustment of conflicting views. The Axis powers challenge these foundations of civilised life.

To all right-thinking men, the issues of this war are quite clear. There are some who believe that this war is a conflict between rival imperialisms, and that there is not much difference between the Allies and the Axis powers. But the little difference there is, is vital and important. In the actual world, the distinction between good and evil is not clear-cut. We do not find there black and white, but things imperceptibly shade from one to the other. While the British system has not been consistent with regard to its ideals of democracy and justice, they would be altogether extinguished if the Dictators won. The problem for the politician is a choice of evils, and political wisdom consists in perceiving how much of an evil it is necessary to tolerate lest worse evil befall. There are many injustices in the British system which are corrupting but that should not betray us into blurring the distinction between unfulfilled justice and a clean negation of justice. Every individual is obliged to choose one rather than the other. Even for those who suffer from the injustices of the British system, the duty is clear. It is to defend the cause of Britain and at the same time assist Britain to remedy the injustices which are manifestly inconsistent with her professed ideals. The failure to live up to these ideals is part of the cause of the present war.

The finest anti-Nazi material is in India, and it is nothing short of a tragedy that she is still mainly unreconciled. If freedom of all people is the aim of this war, as it should be, then those who were conquered in the past must be set free. To win the war will not mean much if it does not remove the great wrongs of the present world. We must demonstrate even to the enemy that we reverence the ideals of

justice and freedom which we condemn him for
rejecting. British statesmen do not seem to realise
sufficiently that new forces are at work which require
a new outlook and interpretation. We need not doubt
that the present Government contains as high an
average of ability as was ever found in a British
Cabinet. Its members, however, are fitted more to
carry on traditional administration than appreciate
new factors or initiate new policies. The Prime
Minister, who is bending all his indisputable genius
and prodigious energies to the supreme task of winning the war has, in spite of his boldness and vision,
become a specialist and is studiously reticent on the
Indian question. The other members belong to an
era that has passed.

The position of Britain in the world has radically
changed. The old policy of slow compromise and fine
adjustment is out of date. New, strange, inconsequent
forces are at work upsetting the old calculations.
Statesmen cast in the old form with their servility to
established institutions are not adequate to the new
conditions. Those who are in charge of India have
the traditional virtues of dignity, honour, efficiency
and even selflessness. They are most competent
members of traditional Government, but are too
firmly set in the old ways to be useful in the new
world. They are immensely intelligent but highly
insensitive. Otherwise it is impossible to understand
a policy which does not countenance the establishment
of a popular government, which does not trust the
leaders of the people with the task of building up the
neglected defences of India, and organising aircraft

and shipbuilding industries in the country. The sands
are running out. Will British statemen take courage
and give content to the noble phrases they utter, and
weld together, in a great democratic federation India
and Britain for mutual service and the service of the
world?

If the new spirit has not captured the imagination
of the British people, if they persist in their old
policies, this war will be a sheer disaster to mankind.
History reveals to us how wars cannot be avoided, so
long as justice is not practised by man to man, by
State to State, unless we accept the principle that the
weak have rights against the strong. Unfortunately,
however, from early times the powerful exacted what
they could and the weak granted what they must.
Thucydides reports that when the people of Melos
appealed to the Athenians, who had them at their
mercy, to spare them, the Athenians would only say,
"Of our gods we believe—and of men we know—that
by a law of their nature wherever they can rule they
will. This law was not made by us, and we are not the
first who have acted upon it, we did but inherit it,
and we shall bequeath it to all time, and we know that
you and all mankind—if you were as strong as we are
—would do as we do." If that is human nature, if
success and failure are the sole measures of right and
wrong, then every excess of fraud, force, and ruthlessness and cruelty is justified, and we cannot complain
if nations play the international game by the rules of
power politics. Unless we defeat this mentality we
might win the war but we would lose the cause. In a
great book—*The City of God*—St. Augustine asks:

"Take away justice, and what are the kingdoms of the earth but great bands of robbers?"

Of this war the end will be the beginning. If we are not to drift into another disastrous display of brute force, moral principles must inspire the peacemakers. It will not be easy; for as Señor de Madariago said: "A democracy that goes to war, if beaten, loses its liberty at the hands of its adversary; if victorious, it loses its liberty at its own hands." A democracy cannot wage war and remain a democracy. It may be said that it gives up its principle only for the duration of the war, and returns to it when victory is won. It is not quite so simple. It would be to take an external and superficial view of democracy, which is a way of life and not a mere political arrangement. We cannot organise for war and yet give full liberty of speech and expression. Herd emotions of fear and anger are bound to be produced, and all the powerful agencies of the press, the radio, and mass demagogy will be utilised for the ostensible purpose of strengthening the will to victory, and these emotions, sedulously cultivated during the war, are likely to endure after it, and increase the difficulties of peace. It requires a supreme effort of reason and imagination to produce the psychological conditions for a just and enduring peace. If the war is to be won on the battlefields, the peace must be defended in universities and seats of learning, by priests, prophets and philosophers; we must train men's minds for a new world where the doctrine of non-violence is not the impracticable dream that it is now supposed to be.

XI

JAYAPRAKASH NARAYAN

> The fame of Jayaprakash Narayan has the ring of a rumour. It is spread everywhere and is so strange that one is tempted to take it with a pinch of salt. He amalgamates in his person an atmosphere of Karl Marx, Shivaji, and the Scarlet Pimpernel.
>
> D. B. DHANAPALA

Introduction

MANY NATIONALIST LEADERS, including Ghose and Nehru, were the products of British universities and training, but Jayaprakash Narayan (1901–   ) shares with Lala Lajpat Rai a background of American experience. While the latter's sojourn in the United States was essentially an interlude of exile, following a successful career, Narayan's future was shaped by his classes at the University of California, which he entered in 1922, and by his studies at other

American universities.[1] He became a Marxist and joined the American Communist Party. After nearly eight restless, hectic years spent in wandering about the land of Harding and Coolidge as farm laborer, mechanic, factory worker, and student, he returned in 1929 to his native India bursting with socialist doctrines and hopes.[2]

Gandhi and Nehru were impressed by the young Communist, and Nehru requested him to establish the Labour Research Department of the Indian National Congress. Here he met other young radicals whom he helped to persuade of the necessity for economic reform and socialism as an integral part of the independence movement. Here was another version of the old Tilak-Gokhale struggle. Eventually, it led to a break with Gandhi's position and the founding in 1934 of the Congress Socialist Party as a party within the Indian National Congress itself. Narayan was the organizing secretary. Several of the leaders remained high in the councils of the Congress Party, where they attempted to stimulate opposition to British policies and to promote socialist ideology.[3]

The most dramatic phase of Narayan's career occurred during the Second World War, when he quickly antagonized the British by protesting against the use of Indian resources "to buttress up imperialism and to be converted through the process of war into the chains of the country's slavery." [4] He was imprisoned, but in November, 1942 he made a sensational break from the Hazari Bagh Jail, scaling the high walls with ropes. Despite the intensive search carried on by police and military, despite the price put on his head, he moved about India in disguise, organizing his underground resistance movement. By the time he was finally re-arrested he had become something of a legend.

But as early as 1940 he had broken with his old associates, and at the Socialist Party convention, in 1949, he pleaded for "democratic socialism." More and more, after Gandhi's death, he thought and argued in Gandhian terms. A further shift in outlook developed from his contact with Vinoba Bhave and the Bhoodan program. He revised his estimate of human motivation, stressing the role of individual character as against government organization and economic legislation. In 1954 he retired publicly from party politics and announced his support of the Sarvodaya ideal. He commended the example of Gandhi.

He would agree with Suresh Ramabhai's comment: "Gandhiji did not touch the ruling machinery even with a pair of tongs. If law could bring grist to the mill of the people, he would have certainly accepted office. Law cannot be instrumental in changing socio-economic values or outlook towards life. That is impossible without a basic change—change at the root." [5] This theme Narayan develops in the following discussion on the relationship between morality and politics.

Social and
Human Reconstruction

BY JAYAPRAKASH NARAYAN

In days gone by men tried to be good, impelled by
some higher moral force in which they believed;
and goodness meant such things as truthfulness, honesty, kindness, chastity, unselfishness. Men felt that it
was the highest moral duty to try to be good. Whether
they succeeded in their trial, or whether they tried at
all, was a different matter. The important point is
that society provided every individual with the motive
to be good: it was the command of religion, of God;
it was necessary for one's highest growth, for self-
realisation; it brought peace and supreme happiness;
it brought salvation and freedom from births and
deaths.

In present society, with the hold of religion gone,
faith in God shaken, moral values discarded as dead-
weights of the dark ages of history; in short, with
materialism enthroned in men's hearts, are there any
incentives to goodness left? Indeed, has the question
any relevance at all to present facts, problems and
ideals of human society?

Social and Human Reconstruction

I hold emphatically that no other question is more relevant to us today.

In spite of what may be broadly described as the materialist climate of present society, men everywhere are engaged, in their different ways, in creating a heaven upon earth—in remaking, refining, perfecting human society. These efforts, even the most idealistic and ambitious, such as Communism of its original conception, seem, however, to be shipwrecking on one obdurate rock—human baseness. It is clearer today than ever that social reconstruction is impossible without human reconstruction. Society cannot be good unless individual men are good, and particularly those men who form the elite of society.

Here then is the crux of the modern problem. Men wish to create, if not an ideal, at least a good society. Modern science and technology make that task far easier than ever before. But men lack the tools with which to make themselves. And the ideals are forgotten, and they begin to fight for power, position, spoils, bringing down the whole edifice of the new society.

Therefore, the problem of human goodness is of supreme moment today. The individual asks today why he should be good. There is no God, no soul, no morality, no life hereafter, no cycle of birth and death. He is merely an organism of matter, fortuitously brought into being, and destined soon to dissolve into the infinite ocean of matter. He sees all around him evil succeed—corruption, profiteering, lying, deception, cruelty, power—politics, violence. He asks naturally why he should be virtuous. Our social norms of today and the materialist philosophy which rules the affairs of men answer back: he need not. The cleverer he is, the more gifted, the more courageously he practises the new amorality, and in the toils of this amorality the dreams and aspirations of human-kind become warped and twisted.

For many years I have worshipped at the shrine of the goddess—Dialectical Materialism—which seemed to me intellectually more satisfying than any other philosophy. But while the main quest of philosophy remains unsatisfied, it has become patent to me that materialism of any sort robs man of the means to become truly human. In a material civilization man has no rational incentive to be good. . . . I feel convinced, therefore, that man must go beyond the material to find the incentives to goodness. As a corollary, I feel further that the task of social reconstruction cannot succeed under the inspiration of a materialist philosophy.

It may be asked if any social conditioning is at all necessary for men to acquire goodness. Is not man essentially good? Are not most men in every society decent?

Yes and no.

Man is a socio-organic being: He is partly the product of "nature" and partly that of society. What man is by nature cannot be said with certainty. Indeed, the very concepts of good and bad are supernatural or super-organic. There is nothing good or bad in nature. Human nature, apart from the instincts of self and race preservation, is most likely of a neutral character which acquires moral tones in accordance with social conditioning.

It is true that in every society most men are decent and good. These men go through life without being called upon to make any vital moral judgments. Their routine of life runs within narrow circles, and custom and tradition answer for them the questions concerning right and wrong.

But, firstly, these harmless decent men are apt under social stimuli to turn suddenly wild and vicious.

Secondly, what is vital for the character of society, and for the direction of its growth, is not so much the character of the inert mass as that of the elite. It is the philosophy and action of this group of the select that determine the destinies of men. To the extent the elite becomes godless or amoral, to that extent evil overtakes the human race.

Let me hasten to remove a possible misunderstanding. I do not mean to suggest that all those who profess a philosophy of materialism are vicious nor that all non-materialists are good. But what I do assert is that there is no logic in materialism for the individual to endeavour deliberately to acquire and practise goodness. On the other hand, those who go beyond matter will find it difficult to justify non-good.

Non-materialism—I am using this negative phrase because I have no particular school in mind—by rejecting matter as the ultimate reality, immediately elevates the individual to a moral plane, and urges him, without reference to any objective outside of himself, to endeavour to realise his own true nature and fulfil the purpose of his being. This endeavour becomes the powerful motive force that drives him in its natural course to the good and the true. It will be seen as an important corollary of this that only when materialism is transcended does individual man come into his own and become an end in himself.

. . . We all want to change the structure of our society. We would like to build up Sarvodaya Society as soon as possible. The problem is: how are we to build such a Sarvodaya Society in our country? If Gandhiji had been here he would have shown us the way. Under his leadership we all worked and fought for our independence. But ever since we achieved independence, Gandhiji's own disciples have constituted the Government of the country. Ever since then I have been thinking whether it is possible to build up a society of Gandhiji's conception, through law, through political power, through political leadership.

After independence the whole country looked towards Delhi. I do not know how many of you believe that building up of a Sarvodaya Society is possible through the State power. But, so far as I am concerned, I have more and more realised and I am now convinced that the way of looking towards Delhi was not Gandhiji's way. There we find the prevalent practice of Democracy. There is the ruling party, there is the Opposition, there are elections, there is the rule by majority and all the rest of it. But the people have realised that through State power and legal methods we cannot build Sarvodaya Society. Maybe the State Power can build up a Socialist society. It certainly cannot make real the conception of Sarvodaya on this earth.

Then the question remains: how is Sarvodaya Society to be built up? Who will constitute the vanguard? What is the way? Maybe law will trail behind, but then who will be moving in the front?

Till a few years ago we all used to swear by the constructive programme. After independence, constructive work went into the background. Constructive workers thought that they would move behind the Government and would carry on items like spinning, Nai Talim etc.[6] But in his heart of hearts no constructive worker believed that through this method the society would be changed. Instances may be found of villages where spinning and Nai Talim etc., were completely implemented. But that did not mean an iota of change in the social structure of the village. Naturally, therefore, there was confusion and disillusionment and the problem remains unsolved for the constructive workers today as before. The problem stands even today. Not that there have been no attempts to answer these questions. Viewpoints have been put forward. But the ideas are not yet clear. There are people in the administration also who fully subscribe to the Sarvodaya point of view. Even they, apparently, are not able to do much by way of building up Sarvodaya Society.

Thinking over all these questions, I have come to certain conclusions. . . . I know that a number of friends say Jayaprakash changes his views very quickly, that he has been doing that all his life, that nobody can say today what Jayaprakash will be tomorrow. I would certainly admit that my views have changed from time to time. But I must also confess that throughout, a fire has been continuously burning in my heart. I have always felt a great urge to change the present society which is based on injustice and exploitation. We will have to build up a new society where there will be equality and fullest freedom.

We have always desired that changes should come in our society as soon as possible. All these years this conviction was growing deeper within me that our object can be achieved only through Sarvodaya. That feeling was growing. But I was probing for the way, for the path, to reach the goal. And the path became increasingly clearer to me as the Bhoodan movement developed.[7] So, finally at Bodh-Gaya I decided to leave politics and devote myself to this work. I feel that all people who believe in Sarvodaya ideals should take a similar course.

The position is very clear. If through State power we cannot build Sarvodaya, if a non-violent revolution in our society is not possible through the administrative machinery, then what other alternative remains before us for building up a new society? Thinking and ever thinking over this question, I have arrived at some conclusions. I feel that the path of changing society in accordance with Mahatmaji's ideals is an entirely new one, which has hitherto not been attempted in the world. And working upon the premises laid down by the Father of the Nation, Vinobaji has successfully reduced it to a science.

What can be the method of pushing forward the viewpoint of truth, and what can be the method of mass Agraha (insistence)? Vinobaji has placed before us his ideas on Bhoodan and Sampattidan which are meant only for pushing forward this conception.[8] I feel that there is no path better than this. The basic question is not how much land we got in Bhoodan. The important thing is that this point of view is being more and more accepted, that land belongs to society, that property belongs to no individual. Bhoodan and Sampattidan have a tremendous revolutionary significance because they non-violently make their way forward and the principles are being increasingly accepted by Indian society. No doubt our views can be propagated through pamphlets and speeches. But, as long as that propaganda is not accompanied by actual movement which affects the lives of the people, till then no movement for social transformation can achieve a mass character.

I am reminded of the Salt Satyagraha.[9] When Gandhiji struck upon the novel method, there were many who pooh-poohed and laughed at it. But that small Salt Satyagraha transformed the entire Nation. Indian people, who were afraid of the mighty British Empire, got courage and became fearless. More or less the same role is being played to-day by the Bhoodan movement in transforming the society. As far as the question of transformation of Indian society is concerned, there are a lot of people who think well of the Bhoodan movement. I would tell them that if they think that Bhoodan is just one of the scores of other works being done in this country, then they have not fully understood its implications.

If you consider that Bhoodan is just one of the scores of other activities then nothing is going to materialize. Not that other activities are bad or un-important. We will have to put all our energy into this Bhoodan work. We will have to jump into it with all our energies, just as in times of revolution. We have to bring about this revolution in the minds and thoughts in every one in all homes and villages of our motherland. We have to make every one realise that an economic revolution has to take place in our society. For the masses of our people economic factors are the most dominant. That is why Vinobaji has taken up the economic issue with a view to change the society, and has been telling us how there exists a non-violent way of solving the economic problems.

Friends, after having given my deepest thought to the subject during the last four years, I gathered the necessary enthusiasm and courage to place these views before you. I would call upon all of you to leave every other activity and function, and jump into this great task of bringing about a non-violent revolution in our society. This is a non-violent revolution with main emphasis on cottage industries, to be brought about through Bhoodan.

Nobody will dispute that to establish a non-violent society we should believe in non-violence. What is the significance of Bhoodan? Why has that been made the centre of all other activities? The question arises because we have realised that the old items of constructive programmes are not effective in bringing about a non-violent revolution. There are villages which have spun on Charkha regularly for the last 25 years but there has been no transformation in the set up of these villages.[10] Those who spun might have got some cash, but there came no revolution in the village life. Nai Talim also has been implemented in some villages. It has failed to bring about any change in the people. The Bhoodan movement has been progressing during the last four years. We have received over 35 lakhs of acres. In Orissa over 100 villages have been fully donated to the Bhoodan movement, which means that in these 100 villages at least the land revolution is complete. The inhabitants of these villages have given up their property rights over land.

Experience has shown, and will show, that to the extent the Bhoodan movement advances, to that extent all other constructive activities advance and the creative capacities of our masses will develop. Actually speaking, I visualise so many things to be done once Bhoodan movement is complete. But we have not enough workers to cope with the task.

The main idea is that we should bring about a revolution in people's thoughts. That is not likely to take place through enactments, through legislatures. We have at last got at a point where we can take a final stand and that is the idea of Bhoodan and Sampattidan. Here is an opportunity for every one to take some part if he is willing to leave his property rights fully, or if he cannot do that, partly. Thus revolutionary ideas spread through the country.

There is a great difference between violent revolution and non-violent revolution. The latter is entirely dependent upon mobilising the sanction of the enlightened masses. In a scheme of non-violent revolution, greatest emphasis is upon changing the views of the people and their methods of behavior in society. In a violent revolution it is the power of the State, with all its vast appendages, which plays a decisive role. . . .

The conclusion is obvious. It is not possible to achieve any success through developing the power of the State. The real method lies in developing the power of the masses, and their moral strength. We have before us the slogan of Welfare State. I would like the Sarvodaya workers to fully understand the various concepts which seem to be jumbled up in this much talked of Welfare State. It is a slow-moving conception of changing society into a Socialistic one.

But our Bhoodan movement is not merely one among the many other numerous activities. It is the work today. Vinobaji first got the inspiration. He has become the means for the change. God has chosen him for this task. Whatever it may be, I must say that revolution cannot be accomplished by work at leisure. If we want revolution we will have to work with quick speed. That is why I say to those who are in the administration, and who in their heart of hearts believe in the Sarvodaya ideals, to leave the administration and join the movement and work actively in it. Similarly, I would call upon the constructive workers to lock up their shops for the present and to leave all other constructive activities and to jump straight into this movement.

XII

VINOBA BHAVE

As I watched Vinoba, I understood for the first
time what a powerful force is employed when a
moderate begins conducting a revolution, when an
individual walks quietly among millions and is able
to command by whispers.

J. H. Noyes

Introduction

For some years after the death of Gandhi,
early in 1948, many in the Western world mourned
his passing as a near-fatal blow to the nonviolent
Satyagraha movement which he had so ably led.
Jawaharlal Nehru, despite his loyalty to Gandhi,
frankly questioned certain aspects of his theory; the
administration of independent India used force in
the Hyderabad dispute and in Kashmir, though in
both instances such measures were considered as

legitimate police measures; the program of social reconstruction would require use of coercion by government; and the first purpose of the Satyagraha movement had already been achieved with independence, leaving little incentive to support its disciplines of sacrifice and self-restraint. With Gandhi gone and no successor in sight, the nonviolent method of revolution seemed destined to become but an interlude in the history of twentieth-century India.

Then from the dusty fields of central India, news dispatches began reaching the outside, telling of the work of a slender Brahman who had walked tirelessly down the jungle roads, village to village, preaching a doctrine called *Sarvodaya*. He had walked fearlessly into the Telangana country, swept for months by terror and in the grip of an armed uprising. He had visited terrorists in the jails and in the hills and had talked to them of Nonviolence and the Gandhian way.

But this leader was no stranger to Indians. Gandhi himself had sponsored him as the first Satyagrahi to offer nonviolent resistance to the British in the campaign of October 1940, Nehru having been chosen as the second. Years before, he had enlisted as one of the members of Gandhi's Ashram at its commencement. The older man's admiration for his pupil was boundless: "He is, next to me, the best exponent and embodiment of non-violence. I use the words 'next to me' because he has taken the cult of non-violence from me . . . He has greater power of concentration than myself. His antipathy of war is born of pure non-violence." [1]

Actually, Vinoba Bhave (1895–   ) was endowed with some impressive capacities. He was a Sanskrit scholar, and he had mastered, in addition to his native Marathi, English, Hindi, Gujarati, Arabic and other languages—about eighteen in all. He had an intimate knowledge of the Hindu classics and had written commentaries on several of them. He was a skilled mathematician.

In all these gifts he resembled the earlier Maratha genius, Bal Gangadhar Tilak. It was, in fact, the latter's Marathi weekly, *Kesari*, that first inspired Vinoba's scholarship and dedication to public service. He says of it, "When I was nine I developed a passion for *Kesari* . . . I studied articles in it on every conceivable topic and it laid the foundation of practically all my learning." [2]

The *Sarvodaya* which he preached was a product of Gandhi's encounter with John Ruskin. In his autobiography, Gandhi wrote, "Of these books, the one that brought about an instantaneous and practical transformation in my life was *Unto This Last*. I translated it later into Gujarati, entitling it 'Sarvodaya' (The Welfare of All)." [3] He understood Sarvodaya to mean that the good of the individual is dependent upon the good of all and that all work, high or low, is of equal value. He went further and proclaimed the life of labor—farming and handicraft—as the best.

Vinoba's application of this principle was embodied in a land program known as the *Bhoodan Yajna* or Land Gifts Mission. He has said, "My aim is to bring about a threefold revolution . . . I want to prevent a violent revolution and bring about instead a non-violent revolution. The future peace and prosperity of the country depends upon the peaceful solution of the land problem." [4] In pursuit of his mission he has become known as the "Walking Saint," having literally walked tens of thousands of miles and collected several million acres of land from large and small holders for distribution to the landless.[5]

Vinoba's appeal is strictly nonviolent. "If you want to loot the people," he tells the violent, "loot, as I do with love and affection." [6] He pleads with landholders to treat him as a "sixth son" and give over to him one-sixth of their holdings. When a single owner in a village succumbs to the power of Bhave's quiet insistence, others are inspired or shamed into following suit and the process of voluntary land distribution proceeds apace. Critics have questioned the economic wisdom of dividing parcels which may already be too small for efficient operation or too barren for tillage without large capital expenditures. But the "Walking Saint" is seemingly undisturbed. He would go further and do away with all private ownership of land in favor of community ownership and development. A program of "Gramdan" or pooling of community resources would make possible a society of peasant cooperatives.[7] The government of India has given serious attention to the possibilities of social reform through the Bhoodan movement and Nehru has openly supported the program. Bhave has thus carried on the mission of reform which originally coupled with Swaraj in the political objectives of Ranade and other early Congress leaders.

The following talk by Vinoba, given at Warangal, Hyderabad, early in his walking campaign to inaugurate the land-gift program, describes the motives and methods of the noted spokesman of Sarvodaya.[8] It demonstrates clearly that such leaders did not consider India's problems to be solved with the achievement of independence. Bhoodan was a continuation of earlier ideals of reform.

The Path of Love

BY VINOBA BHAVE

Though humanity has been in existence for thousands of years, for centuries groups of men remained so unknown to one another that they, owing to inadequate means of travelling and communication, often believed they were the only people living on the earth. The extent of the world was also imperfectly known. Events as catastrophic as the late Assam earthquake might happen in one part of the world without the people in another part becoming in the least aware of them. With the growth of knowledge, man's knowledge both of nature and of other groups of men, increased. The contact was many sided—physical, mental, religious, spiritual, cultural, political, etc. It was not always happy; at times it was very bitter. But I believe that on the whole, the result was good.

Examples of this might be cited from all parts of the world. The confluence of the Aryans and the Dravidians in India is an example nearer home. It was a meeting of the mountain civilization of the North and of the sea civilization of the South. They had lived unknown to one another for thousands of years. When they met, they had both war and peace, segregation and mixture. Both had their independently developed separate cultures. The Aryans were more intellectual and the Dravidians more devotional. Their confluence ultimately produced a big nation, in which the good points of both the North and the South were absorbed. But this new culture, too, later on proved to be imperfect.

In course of time came the Muslims with their own civilization, and there was a conflict between the old and this newcomer. The Muslim civilization in its expansion seems to have followed two different methods: one of violence and destruction, the other of love and construction. Gazni and Aurangzeb are examples of the first; Akbar and Kabir, those of the second.

But Islam filled a deficiency in the Indian culture. It regarded all men as equal. Although this principle was recognized in the Upanishads, it was not visible in our social order; the principle had not been acted upon. Islam put the principle into practice. The Indian culture, with its mutually exclusive castes, came into conflict with the casteless civilization of Islam, and history records the progress and the result

191

of that conflict. None can say that Islam conquered India on the battlefield. But before the Muslim soldier came with his sword, the Muslim fakir (saint) had come with his teachings, and he wandered from village to village and gave a message which was attractive.

At the same time India also produced a number of preachers who attacked caste divisions and laid special emphasis on the unity of God. No doubt, Islam had a great share in it. It is a valuable contribution of Islam to Indian culture. Thus with the addition of Islam a new compound of Indian civilization was produced.[9]

Then came the Europeans about three hundred years ago, attracted by the wealth of India and stimulated by the spirit of the Renaissance, which ultimately produced, among other things, the advance of modern science and the industrial revolution. As a matter of fact, at the time when the Europeans came here, India was far more ahead of Europe in science, industry, philosophy, etc. She was also far more prosperous. Once again the meeting of the two civilizations was both bitter and sweet. Indian civilization was tremendously affected, and in fact a new compound is in the process of formation. A new way of living and thinking has been introduced. The new thought-currents, like Socialism, Communism, etc., have arrived from the West and they have come to stay.

Necessarily there is a struggle between the two. I believe that ultimately Indian culture will lose nothing thereby. The scum will be washed off, and a new compound culture will be produced. I say this because in spite of a great import of new ideas and knowledge from the West, India has not ceased to produce profound original teachers, thinkers and investigators all along. Of course, in the present formative stage, we witness both good and evil.

Though I had not directly attended to the Communist problem of Hyderabad so far, ever since Gandhiji's death I had been watching it and keeping myself informed of its violent developments. I confess that incendiary and murderous activities, painful as they were, did not unnerve me, because I know that the birth of a new culture has always been accompanied with blood-baths in the past, and hence there is nothing new in it. What is needed is not to get panicky, but to keep our heads cool and find peaceful means of resolving the conflict.

The Government have kept a special police force in Telangana to restore peace. Policemen are not expected to think out and institute reforms. They can only use their arms and strike terror. If it were a question of clearing a forest of tigers, their employment would be quite useful. But here they have to deal with human beings, however mistaken and misguided. There is a new idea and a goal behind these activities, and where a new idea is born mere repression cannot combat it. Not that the Government do not understand this; but they have a responsibility to protect life and property, and so I do not blame them for the measures employed by them.

But I had all along been seeking a better remedy. I thought that a tour through the district was essen-

tial to seek it. But I wondered how I should do it.
Tour develops thought. But the tour which does that
is not the one undertaken in modern times through
motor cars, railway trains and aeroplanes. In olden
days horses and camels were considered to be the
swiftest conveyances. They could cover as many as
two hundred miles in a night in an emergency. But
teachers like Buddha, Mahavir, Kabir, Nanak, Nama-
dev, Chaitanya preferred to go on foot in order to
deliver their messages far and wide. Thought becomes
clear, mature and remodelled while you walk.

This happened to me as I walked to Shivarampalli
from Wardha. All the way I was seeking a solution of
the problem which the Communists tried to solve in
their own way. One day, the story of the Vaman incarnation flashed through my mind, and Brahman
that I was, I took it up and commenced begging gifts
of land.[10]

I was not confident of the result. How can a few
drops of nectar sweeten a sea? But God put strength
into my words. Somehow people understood the spirit.
They realized that the events that were happening
would bring a revolution in their life, which was beyond the capacity of Governments. They began to
give free gifts of land, at times beyond my expectation.
For instance, at one place 80 acres of land were
needed for Harijans and a single landowner gave one
hundred. A landowner of Nalgunda, who had donated
50 acres already, later on gave 500 following a settlement of his family dispute. It was a fourth of his
total share.

But this is a mere beginning and a gesture. The

spirit must·spread and catch all possessors of property. A gift of a few acres out of a thousand cannot solve the whole problem. Moreover, it is not a problem of one or two districts; it is not even the problem of India alone. It is a world problem—a revolutionary programme. And when a revolution in the way of life is contemplated, it must take place in the mind. The mere material gift of a hundred acres out of ten thousand cannot be sufficient. As a friend and well-wisher of both the rich and the poor, I could feel happy only if I could make the rich look upon the poor as members of their own family. I desired them to consider how they would take the birth of one more son to them. Suppose an owner of 10,000 acres has four sons, and a fifth is born later. Would he not have to make five shares of his property instead of four? I asked the landholders to regard me as an additional heir born to them, and give me my share for the benefit of the poor.

A psychological change like this cannot be brought about by war and violent revolution. It can be brought about only by the methods of Buddha, Christ, Ramanuja and other great teachers.

Ultimately it has to be the dedication of one's all for the wellbeing of all. Those who have must look upon those who have not as a mother looks upon her hungry child. She feeds it before she feeds herself; she starves before she allows it to starve. Let those who possess the strength, skill and knowledge of producing wealth, or the power of holding it, dedicate them to the service of the poor. I desire that the love necessary for doing this is generated in the heart of every one.

I had an interview with some of the Communists in the jail at Warangal. One of the questions which they put to me was to the following effect: "Do you want to resettle the rich in their old homes? Do you think that their hearts have changed? They simply deceive you." I did not discuss these questions there because I had gone there only to study their minds. But here is my faith. If God dwells in the hearts of all beings, and controls every movement of theirs, even their breathing, and if He is the source of all inspiration, a change of heart is always possible. The Lord of the Age is eternally present, and if He desires a change, that change has to be. When a man falls into a stream, it is not only his own capacity of swimming, but also the force of the current that helps him, and it does so whether he likes it or not. Similarly, when the current of the age goes this way, it will help him in changing his heart. In our present world, burning with discord and quarrels, if God desires to sprinkle a few drops of love through me I shall gladly be His instrument. I took lands even from the poor. At one place a person owning only one acre of land donated a *guntha* (1/40th of an acre). I was asked what I would do with such small pieces of land. I said, I would ask the owner to till that *guntha* as a trustee, and utilize the produce for the benefit of the poor. That a man who owns only one acre is prompted to part with a *guntha* out of it is certainly a revolution. It is an ideological revolution, and where there is an ideological revolution, life marches towards progress. Our country has produced men who have renounced large kingdoms as if they were worthless straw.

Thought-force has no limitations. The light of a new idea often brings about a radical change in a man's life. We have seen great men, the power of whose thoughts has transformed the lives of others. It was with this idea of igniting the spark of thought in others that I accepted even small donations. And when Vaman-like I accepted land from the rich, God blessed and assured them that they need no longer run away to the cities to save their lives. It meant that by accepting lands from them, I generated a healthy thought in their minds. There are good and evil thoughts in the minds of every one. And when a good thought enters the mind, it starts a struggle with evil thoughts. Ultimately, the good thought wins. It might take time, but there is no reason to think that the donors are hypocrites. I grant that these donors must have committed many acts of injustice, in coming by the thousands of acres of land. How is it possible for an individual to acquire so much land justly? But in the hearts of even these people, there will now start a struggle and they will begin to think of the injustices they have committed. God will grant them wisdom and they will give up doing wrong. This is how a change of heart takes place in man.

The time has come when we should enlarge our hearts and part with our belongings to others. Giving is a divine weapon. Base weapons cannot stand before it. They melt away before it, because they are made of selfishness, and not of universality or equality, like a divine weapon.

When a gift is given, we may hope that it will generate purity of mind, motherly love, feelings of brotherhood and friendliness and love for the poor. When a person begins to feel concerned for another, a feeling of equality manifests itself, and feelings of hatred and enmity are unable to survive. Enmity has no absolute existence. Like light, virtue is power, a positive substance. Sin is like darkness, without any power of its own. It is negative—absence of substance. Carry light to age-long darkness and the latter will disappear in no time. Similarly when virtue makes its appearance, hatred and enmity cannot exist in its presence. This Bhoodan Yajna (Land-gifts Mission) is an application of Non-violence, an experiment in transformation of life itself. I am only an instrument in the hands of Him, who is the Lord of all ages, like even those who give and those who will receive the gifts. It is a phenomenon inspired by God. For how otherwise can people, who fight even for a foot of land, be inspired to give away hundreds of acres of land freely? My appeal to all and everywhere is to take this as a thing which God desires them to do, and bequeath their lands to the landless liberally and lovingly.

Let me repeat in this connection what I said once before. Non-violence is not opposed to science; it wants fully to avail itself of it. Science can transform this earth into heaven. It can do so only in combination with non-violence. If science and violence are joined together, the world will be shattered to pieces.

There was a time when issues were decided by war in the form of duels. But the age of duels is gone. War began with duels; but the system did not work; so thousands began to fight against thousands; and

The Path of Love

when even that did not prove enough, lakhs gathered on either side, and each party vied with the other in increasing its number of combatants.[11] And we have reached the time when not lakhs but crores participate in war. The choice now is either to prepare for total war, or abandon violence altogether, and accept non-violence. That alone is the problem man is faced with today. To my Communist friends, I would say, you are committing a murder here and a murder there, with some arson and looting; you come out at night and hide yourselves in the hills during the day; of what avail is all this? If at all you want to fight, you must prepare for a world war. Await it. But so long as you do not make preparations of a big war, wherein crores of lives will have to be destroyed, give up these tactics of petty strifes, and avail yourselves of the right of voting, which you have got. Prepare the people for your ideology. A total world war or pure universal love is the choice, with which science has confronted us today.

To the landholders I say, if you will accept the path of love and Non-violence, you will have to abandon the attachment to land. Otherwise the age of violence which is approaching will destroy not only the land but also those who are occupying it. Let us therefore realize that the problem has been presented to us by God Himself, and let us therefore give and give incessantly.

Six months ago, I had not the least idea that God was going to make me an instrument to do the work for which I am walking now from village to village and door to door. But it seems it was the design of

VINOBA BHAVE

God that this work suggested itself to me spontaneously and also began to bear fruit. Gradually, it has taken such shape that the people have come to feel that this is a very powerful programme which is useful not only to our own country but also to the entire world. The people have realized that it is the call of the age. The call got reflected in my heart also. The result is that after staying at Wardha for about two and a half months after the completion of the Telangana tour, I have again commenced a walking-tour in the course of which I have come to your place.

The mission I have undertaken is an act of devotion and service not only of the poor but also of the rich—of all the people. I have a strong conviction that this work is going to appeal to all. In the course of my begging if I happen to get less land at some place, I do not feel that I have received only a little. On the contrary the feeling with me is that whatever I get is only a *prasad* (a token of grace), and that ultimately God is to give me with His thousands of hands, and the two hands of mine will prove quite useless and inadequate for receiving. The present work is only the preparation of a psychological atmosphere. I do feel at every moment that God's will is working behind the present mission. On this sacred day my first humble prayer to Him is: Let me not mind whether or not people give me land in my mission. Let it be as Thou willest. But let me be Thy humble servant. Destroy my ego, annihilate my separateness and the memory of my name. Let Thy name alone prevail in the world. Free Thy child, from the dross of attachment and hatred lurking in its mind. I

200

solemnly declare I have no other desire left in me.

People ask me when I shall reach Delhi.[12] My answer to them is, I do not know. It all depends upon His will. I am advanced in age and my body has been showing signs of fatigue and exhaustion. This is the only desire of my mind and I feel it constantly. Whenever I get even five minutes' rest or solitude, the only urge uppermost in my mind is that my ego should completely get destroyed. In what language am I speaking today with God? What have I been speaking with the human tongue? I say, "I am experiencing the Presence of Bapu along with that of the Supreme Spirit." [13] Bapu continuously showered his blessings on me. By nature I have been a man of the forest and stranger to ways of civilization. I even dread to meet great people. But nowadays I enter everybody's house unhesitatingly, as did Narada among gods, demons and men.[14] This is all the miracle of Bapu's blessings. I have a conviction that Bapu will be feeling satisfied with my present work from whatever corner of the Universe he may be in.

My dear friends, though I am trying to speak today, it is going to be a difficult task. It will, however, be my attempt to do it as best as I can. Sometimes I reflect about the efficacy of speaking. To what extent does it bear fruit? I shall narrate only yesterday's incident as an illustration.

In a place where I spent the whole day and delivered a speech before the prayer audience, I got only four acres. I returned to my place after the conclusion of the speech, and began my study of the Upanishads, as I have been doing of late. Hardly ten minutes had passed before a villager came to me. He had neither participated in the prayer nor heard my speech. He said, "I have come to donate land." He had come from a distance of six miles. He gave me one acre out of his six. Scarcely had he turned his back, when another villager from a longer distance came and donated fifty-two acres. I began to reflect, who is the inspirer of these donations? I got only four acres, where I spent the day and made a speech. And here are donations without that effort. What is it that influences the minds of people? Why should man need the help of speech? If man's life becomes absolutely pure, not a word will he need to utter. A thought in the heart conceived at home would do the work. But it is a stage, which is yet to come, when God will grant me purity of mind. For the present He makes me go from place to place and inspires me to ask for land donations. I, therefore, speak and beg alms of land for the poor. But not a shadow of doubt there is in my mind that it is not my efforts that will achieve any results. It is only His inspiration that will achieve and is already achieving them.

Though my own stomach is very small, that of the Daridranarayana is very big.[15] So if any one asks me what my demand is I say, "Five crore acres of land." I mean thereby cultivable land. If there are five sons in the family, I want to be considered the sixth; if four, the fifth. Thus I claim one fifth or one sixth of the total cultivable land in the country.

This is no ordinary conventional charity. Giving of land to the poor and the needy is very much more than that. We earn merit if we feed a man even for a single day. When feeding a man for a day is so meritorious, how much more so would be the gift of an acre of land which will feed him for the whole of his life? I, therefore, appeal to all of you to contribute your mite for the worship of Daridranarayana. This is real yajna—sacrifice. I, therefore, beseech every one to come forward and put his shoulder to this task.

This will usher in an unprecedented and mighty revolution in our country. I can, even as I stand here, behold it taking place before my eyes. People talk of the Russian revolution. America presents an example of a revolution of another type.[16] But looking at both these countries, I find that neither type of revolution is in accordance with the genius of India. They are not in accord with our traditions and culture. I firmly believe that India should be able to evolve, consistent with her ideals, a new type of revolution, based purely on love. If people begin to donate lands of their own free will, readily and generously, the whole atmosphere will undergo a sudden change in the twinkling of an eye, and India might well show the way to a new era of freedom, love and happiness for the whole world. This sacrifice embodies this great aspiration and, speaking for myself, I am convinced that this aspiration is going to be fulfilled. I therefore urge all of you, whether you are a member of the Congress, a Socialist, a Praja Party man, or an independent, to ponder over this problem, and realize the value of the Land-gifts Mission. Other things may be left to take their due course, but this one brooks no delay. It is a desideratum to which all must attend. If it is done, India will save herself and the world too, for our action will have trailed a path to freedom and peace which the world may see and tread.

Wherever I go, people speak to me of the rampancy of black-marketing, corruption and bribery. But I do not feel depressed. I do not believe that the heart of India has begun to decay. Nor do I believe that the rich have become corrupt beyond redemption. The sacred ideals and traditions, the spiritual riches which our forefathers have bequeathed to us are certainly more valuable than any material wealth. Hence though there is black-marketing and corruption, yet I do not believe that our people as a whole can be too bad. Therefore we should look for the root of this elsewhere. All this corruption, which we see around us, is due to the evils in the present-day economy. The organization of our economic life is bad. People are swept away by the tide of these outer evils, and led to commit mistakes. Therefore if we can change the structure of the economic life, you may be sure that our people can well set a unique example in the world.

Hence, after Gandhiji's demise, some of us who believe in Sarvodaya formed a brotherhood, Sarvodaya Samaj, in which no one hates anybody. Every one loves every one else. There is no exploitation. I hold to the belief that the moment we succeed in creating a society free from exploitation, the intellectual and spiritual talent of the people of India, which lies obscured at present, will shine forth. We, the believers of Sarvodaya, therefore, have vowed that we will change the present structure of society. I have absolute belief in this mission, otherwise I could not have approached you to give away your lands so openly and unreservedly. I realize that God has rewarded my effort more than I deserve. I have no cause for complaint. All that I have to do is to explain the idea to the people.

XIII

RESPONSE TO THE WEST: THE INDIAN WAY

Your revolution must be bloodless; but that does not
mean that you may not have to suffer or go to jail.

B. G. TILAK

THE PRECEDING ESSAYS demonstrate the complexity of Indian political philosophy during the long
struggle with Western ideas and institutions. At first,
Hindus (especially the University graduates) seem
to have been shamed by what appeared to be the gross
superstition, barbarous customs, ignorance and poverty
in Indian tradition and society. At this stage, Indians
felt that European civilization promised freedom and
power and affluence and sanity. The British were the
transmitters of this progressive culture, and they provided a happy partnership with the Indian peoples

in their national development. Of course, there were some weaknesses, even abuses, in the English administration. But the general arrangement seemed salutary, and it was felt the problems might be resolved by better understanding and reasonable negotiation. Subsequently, however, Hindus, intensely proud of their traditions and institutions, became increasingly critical of Western power and wealth. The latter they held to be admirable in its place, though it had unfortunately been used to enslave and exploit the citizenry of one of the oldest civilizations on earth.

Those Indians who held that earlier view saw reform as the key to national salvation and were willing to pursue reform goals through British institutions. Those who held the latter view saw Swaraj as the essential condition for the solution of all problems.[1]

The above classification, provides an over-simplified picture. Were the whole problem quite that easy to understand and solve, the position of nineteenth- and twentieth-century India would be less baffling than it is. There would be the familiar liberal reformer opposing the traditional conservative. But the reformer is here somehow involved with the foreign exploiter, and the issues become confused. Furthermore, the intense Nationalist is sometimes also an avid reformer. Not all figures are in as sharp contrast as Tilak and Gokhale. And even Gokhale is a sharp critic of the British, while Tilak supports some reforms. There is, however, a gradual shift in emphasis from reform to independence in the whole Nationalist movement, until the clamor for Swaraj overcomes all other forces in the councils of the Congress high command.

Despite the ever sharpening emphasis on independence and the ever heightening friction with the British, the Nationalist movement was, on the whole, a bloodless one. The tragedies of Amritsar and Chauri Chaura, and the brutalities of the salt march and Satyagraha campaigns notwithstanding, the record as a whole is remarkably nonviolent.[2]

How can the consummation of a revolution as sweeping and complex as that which produced Indian Swaraj, which was lacking in the turbulence that marked the American, French, and Russian revolutions, be accounted for? Every element conducive to violence was present—racial and cultural contrasts, economic exploitation, agitation and discontent, international tensions. Yet no bloody convulsion resulted.

To the leadership of the Indian Congress must go the major credit for the course of the Nationalist revolution. Some would say that the person most responsible was Mohandas K. Gandhi. Certainly the importance of his dedication to "harmlessness," together with his hold upon the Indian masses, can hardly be overestimated. But Gandhi was deeply influenced by his Congress predecessors, and they, in turn, were the product of two basic thought currents.

Ultimately, the atmosphere of the independence movement is traceable to the Hindu tradition of Ahimsa and the British tradition of the supremacy of law, which is close in spirit to Indian Dharma.[3] Both elements permeate the writings and speeches of those who led the Congress.

Enthusiasts have called this approach the "Indian Way." Yet one would have a distorted picture of the currents of modern Indian political thought if he lost sight of the persistence and power of the "violent tradition" in India. There is a strain of extreme ruthlessness in the "Arthashastra" literature, in portions of the epic *Mahabharata* and the *Code of Manu*.[4] And despite the well-publicized renunciation of conquest by the emperor Asoka after his victories in 261 B.C., military glory continued to be a major goal of Hindu rulers in succeeding centuries. The ruthlessness of Shivaji, the seventeenth century Maratha chief was eulogized by Tilak in a public meeting as follows: "No blame attaches to any person if he is doing deeds without being actuated by a desire to reap the fruit of his deeds. With benevolent intentions, Sri Shivaji murdered Afzul Khan for the good of others. If thieves enter our house [the reference to British rulers is obvious] and we have not sufficient strength in our wrists to drive them out, we should, without hesitation, shut them up and burn them alive."[5]

During the struggle with the English, bomb throwing and other incidents of terror broke out at various times and places. Even in distant California, U.S.A., armed plots against the Crown were hatched by Indian exiles, during the First World War.[6] The terrible slaughter resulting from Hindu-Moslem clashes in the Punjab and elsewhere, after the partition of India and Pakistan, shows how close to the surface are the violent elements of Indian culture.

Tilak's early editorials and speeches do have a strong flavor of ruthlessness at times; it is nevertheless significant that he chose to deny under oath that he was advocating bloodshed—and he later stated publicly that acts of terrorism served to hinder the progress of the Nationalist movement.[7] Though Aurobindo Ghose was a member of the Bengal terrorists, he abjured all political controversy to become a religious recluse. And while the Japanese example inspired a powerful ferment in India, during the Second World War, even bringing about the creation in Southeast Asia of a so-called "Indian National Army," the fiery movement headed by Subhas Bose was eventually discredited.[8] Even Western ideologies of social upheaval did not prevail against the criticisms of a Gandhi and a Bhave.

The significant fact which emerges is that the Congress leadership, on the whole, chose the nonviolent elements in Indian and English culture to underwrite its program. Was this choice due to the greater power and prevalence of the Ahimsa tradition in India and to the "Rule of Law" in Britain, or was it due to historical accident?—to the fact that the Indian leaders of the nineteenth and twentieth centuries happened to be largely of the temperament of Ranade and Gandhi? Or was Nonviolence simply good strategy and tactics against the overwhelming power of the British rulers?

There is, of course, no positive answer. Most history poses such problems. But the course of Indian thought after Kabir and Tulsidas, and more recently Roy, seems to reveal a strong tendency toward Bhakti and Ahimsa. That is, toward the spirit of compromise and understanding which is in part the product of the *rapprochement* between Moslem and Hindu attitudes after the cruelties of the Moslem conquest and the bigotry of Aurangzeb.[9] On the British side, one cannot deny the power of the concept of legal supremacy and the abhorrence of civil strife as epitomized in Burke's essays on the French Revolution.

Though we may recognize the force of the above traditions, it would leave a false estimate of the Hindu theorists if we did not stress the amazing personal capacities of these Nationalist leaders, all of them products of the Indian Renaissance of the nineteenth century. Writing and speaking in the language of their British conquerors, the Congress leaders have left a literature that remains monumental in its clarity, richness and vigor. Working in an unparalleled ferment of Ancient and Modern, Eastern and Western ideas, they produced philosophies and institutions that are still in growing contention in the forums of modern ideologies.

Despite the atrocities in the Punjab, in the days following partition of India; despite the resort to force later, in the Hyderabad and Kashmir disputes —all legacies of the Partition issue—we are nevertheless able to witness the continuing vigor of Bhave's nonviolent approach to India's political and social problems, long after the consummation of independence.

The effort was conceived as something more than

the mere absence of war. Vinoba Bhave's theme, and Gandhi's before him, was that only Ahimsa provides any real change and that when an individual or a class resorts to violence to overcome abuses it is thereby assured that the abuses will persist with a mere change of actors. Indeed, these two leaders held even this change to be temporary, for the very groups that win quick power by force are all too soon displaced by others and are themselves forced to rejoin the ranks of the exploited. To produce a "permanent" revolution, the Satyagrahis insisted that it was first necessary to bring about a change in attitude and understanding in each individual. "Love" and "Sacrifice" were seen as powerful means in this struggle, "force" and "compulsion" useless. Such would appear to be the response of the leaders of modern India to the challenge of the West.

Whether this response was but a visionary and gentle interlude in an age of world storm or a unique and continuing Indian way of life remains to be seen.

Notes

Short titles are used throughout the notes. Full data for all references will be found in the bibliography.

SOURCES OF CHAPTER EPIGRAPHS

The sources of the quotations used as chapter epigraphs are as follows:

Opposite title page, from Gokhale's 1905 London speech before the New Reform Club, in his *Speeches of Gopal Krishna Gokhale,* p. 941; chapter i, "India Meets the West," from Sarma, *The Renaissance of Hinduism,* p. 67; chapter ii, "Pattern of Conflict," from Lajpat Rai, *Unhappy India,* p. 400; chapter iii, "The Congress," from Gandhi's speech at the second Round Table Conference of 1931, London, quoted in Sitaramayya, *The History of the Indian National Congress,* I, 20; chapter iv, "Ranade," from Chintamani, *Indian Politics Since the Mutiny,* p. 58; chapter v, "Gokhale," from Hoyland, *Gopal Krishna Gokhale,* pp. 30–31; chapter vi, "Tilak," from Chirol, *Indian Unrest,* p. 41; chapter vii, "Lajpat Rai," from Tikekar, *Gandhigrams,* p. 37; chapter viii, "Gandhi," from Kripalani, *Gandhi the Statesman,* p. 1; chapter ix, "Nehru," from Chintamani, *Indian Politics Since the Mutiny,* p. 195; chapter x, "Radhakrishnan," from Dhanapala, *Eminent Indians,* pp. 63, 72; chapter xi, "Narayan," from Dhanapala, *Eminent Indians,* p. 144; chapter xii, "Bhave," from "Vinoba Bhave —The Man and His Mission," by J. H. Noyes, in *Vinoba Bhave,* P. D. Tandon, ed., p. 56; chapter xiii, "Response to the West," from Tilak's speech at Poona, 25 June 1907, in *Bal Gangadhar Tilak—His Writings and Speeches,* p. 75.

NOTES

SOURCES OF QUOTED TEXT MATERIAL

The sources of the excerpts from Indian writers in the text of various chapters are as follows:

Chapter iv, "Ranade," from *The Indian Nation Builders,* I, 12–32; chapter v, "Gokhale," from *Speeches of Gopal Krishna Gokhale,* pp. 937–946; chapter vi, "Tilak," from *Bal Gangadhar Tilak—His Writings and Speeches,* pp. 56–78, 155–169, 391–393 (also from editorial entitled, "The Country's Misfortune," in the Poona newspaper, *Kesari,* May 3, 1908); chapter vii, "Lajpat Rai," from *The Political Future of India,* pp. 181–189; chapter viii, "Gandhi," from *Autobiography,* pp. 501–519; chapter ix, "Nehru," from *Toward Freedom—The Autobiography of Jawaharlal Nehru,* pp. 128–138; chapter x, "Radhakrishnan," from *Education, Politics, and War,* pp. 28–47, 67–91; chapter xi, "Narayan," from *A Picture of Sarvodaya Social Order,* pp. 31–44; chapter xiii, "Bhave," from *Bhoodan Yajna,* pp. 3–18.

CHAPTER I: *India Meets the West*

1. Although Moslem power was not established until the eleventh century, political disintegration in northern India continued after the collapse of Harsha's empire. In southern India, however, classic Indian culture and political systems survived throughout the Moslem conquest, indeed, continued with some vigor right up to the beginning of India's independence.

2. Signed into law in 1956.

3. Article 40, part IV. See Indian Government, *The Constitution of India,* p. 20.

4. See, for instance, M. K. Gandhi's *Young India, 1924–1926,* pp. 604–5.

5. *Ibid.,* pp. 613–615.

6. *Ibid.,* pp. 599–600.

7. Ram Gopal, *Lokamanya Tilak,* p. 234.

8. *Ibid.*, p. 233. The Swadeshi movement supported the use of Indian as against imported goods.

9. *Ibid.*, p. 285. Swaraj: literally "self-rule." For an excellent summary of modern usage of the term, see Bondurant, *Conquest of Violence*, p. 114.

10. Rabindranath Tagore, *Nationalism*, p. 53.

11. Nehru tells how Japanese victories stirred his youthful enthusiasms and caused him to purchase a large number of books on Japan. Jawaharlal Nehru, *Toward Freedom*, p. 29.

12. Swami Vivekananda, *Complete Works*, V, 288.

CHAPTER II: *Pattern of Conflict*

1. Manuel Komroff, ed., *The Travels of Marco Polo*, p. 284.

2. Nalin C. Gangulay, *Raja Ram Mohun Roy*, p. 106.

3. The London *Times*, Nov. 17, 1891, p. 9.

4. W. H. Moreland, and A. C. Chatterjee, *A Short History of India*, p. 430. But Pattabhi Sitaramayya pays tribute to Curzon's vision, courage, and sense of justice in initiating the Ancient Monuments Preservation Act and in punishing British soldiers guilty of criminal offences against Indian civilians; see his *History of the Indian National Congress*, I, 68.

5. Abbé J. A. Dubois, *Hindu Manners, Customs and Ceremonies*, pp. xxiii–xxiv.

6. Sitaramayya, *op. cit.*, I, 101. For material on Sir Surendranath Banerjea, consult his *A Nation in the Making*.

7. See Sarvepalli Radhakrishnan, *Philosophy Eastern and Western*, I, 488; W. E. Duffett, A. R. Hicks, and G. R. Parkin, *India Today*, pp. 16–19.

8. Percival Spear, *India, Pakistan and the West*, p. 80.

9. *Ibid.*, p. 82.

10. Consult, for example, H. S. Jarrett, trans., *Ain-I-Akbari*, Vol. III, Ch. 4, "The Learning of the Hindus."

11. For an account of Dadu's career, consult W. G. Orr, *A Sixteenth Century Indian Mystic.*

12. For a brief summary of Hindu-Moslem cultural differences, see Spear, *op. cit.*, pp. 76–91.

13. For a popular account of the life of Shivaji, consult Dennis Kincaid, *The Grand Rebel.*

14. Bal Gangadhar Tilak, *Bal Gangadhar Tilak, His Writings and Speeches*, p. 50.

15. S. L. Karandikar, *Lokamanya Bal Gangadhar Tilak*, p. vi. Tilak, in the newspaper *Kesari* of the 27th of September 1904, strongly disapproved of the murder of British officials on the ground that "English administration is not arbitrary individual rule. Therefore it is unmanly to incite to the murder of officers." Karandikar, *op. cit.*, p. 205.

16. Sitaramayya, *op. cit.*, I, 380. For a clear analysis of the meaning of Satyagraha and related Gandhian concepts, consult Bondurant, *op. cit.*, especially Chs. II, IV, VI.

17. Jaiprakash Narain, *A Picture of Sarvodaya Social Order*, p. 31.

18. *Ibid.*, p. 2.

19. R. P. Masani, *The Communist Party of India*, p. 24. For a detailed account of Roy's career consult Gene D. Overstreet and Marshall Windmiller, *Communism in India*, especially pp. 44–58.

20. M. N. Roy and K. K. Sinha, *Royism Explained*, p. 12.

21. *Ibid.*, p. 25.

22. *Ibid.*, p. 26.

23. Quoted in M. R. Masani, *op. cit.*, p. 244.

24. Sarvepalli Radhakrishnan, *Kalki*, p. 22. On this problem of democracy in Indian tradition consult Brown, "Traditional Concepts of Indian Leadership," in Richard L. Park and Irene Tinker, eds., *Leadership and Political Institutions in India* (Ch. I).

25. Radhakrishnan, *The Hindu View of Life*, pp. 116–117.

26. For an excellent summary of this attempt consult

Margaret W. Fisher and Joan V. Bondurant, *Indian Approaches to a Socialist Society*.

CHAPTER III: *The Congress*

1. For a concise picture of Hume's life and character see Sitaramayya, *op. cit.*, pp. 77–79.

2. Gladstone himself strongly supported the Congress and was greatly admired by Indians. He also supported freedom for the Indian native press. Sitaramayya, *op. cit.*, p. 80.

3. For a thorough analysis of the role of Bengal in the Independence movement consult Richard Leonard Park, "The Rise of Militant Nationalism in Bengal." Regarding the Bengal Revolution of 1905, he summarizes (p. 3), "Here were posed for the first time in organized form both a demand for political independence for India and a philosophy of action, as well as working institutions, by which such independence could be achieved more rapidly." But he adds (pp. 4–5), "One can say that the Bengal revolutionary movement does not compare as regards political effectiveness either in a qualitative or quantitative sense with the Gandhi-led, non-violent resistance compaigns fostered through the Indian National Congress."

4. Both Jinnah and Gandhi were impressed by Gokhale's ideas, but Jinnah, of course, broke completely with Gandhi and the Congress. In a sense, therefore, Jinnah does not quite belong in the "main line of succession."

5. R. P. Masani, *Dadabhai Naoroji*, p. 9. This entire work is a basic source for the career of Naoroji. For other sources see Sitaramayya, *op. cit.*, I, pp. 83–85; C. Yajneswara Chintamani, *Indian Politics Since the Mutiny*, pp. 20–21, 56–57.

6. A collection of writings under this title was published in 1901, but a smaller volume entitled *Poverty of India* appeared in 1878.

7. He was thereafter dubbed "narrow majority," a nickname that stuck to him for some time. (See R. P. Masani, *op. cit.*, pp. 257–285).

8. Quoted in Sitaramayya, *op. cit.*, I, p. 9.

9. *Loc. cit.*

10. For other actions and activities of this Congress meeting see *ibid.* pp. 18–19. Also consult Berjoy Krishna Bhattacharya, *A Short History of the Indian National Congress;* Hemendranath Dasgupta, *Indian National Congress.*

11. Regarding Ranade's position in public affairs during this period, see Banerjea, *A Nation in the Making*, p. 139.

12. Sitaramayya, *op. cit.*, I, 97.

13. For subsequent Home Rule activities, see D. V. Tahmankar, *Lokamanya Tilak*, pp. 250–258.

14. See Sitaramayya, *op. cit.*, I, 125. In 1916, Tilak rejoined the Congress, at Lucknow, for the first time since the Surat split. On this occasion, even Moslems worked harmoniously with Hindus.

15. Sitamarayya, *op. cit.*, II, 611. When the Viceroy, Lord Hardinge, narrowly escaped death in 1912 from a bomb thrown at him in Delhi, the Congress from Patna sent him a telegram expressing "sorrow and indignation at the outrage." (Sitamarayya, *op. cit.*, I, 73). For the comments of another Nationalist, consult the Bengali leader, Bipin Chandra Pal, *Memories of My Life; Nationality and Empire; Swaraj*. In the last of these Pal opposes armed revolt on the ground that it would "only be able to replace present foreign autocracy by a native autocracy."

CHAPTER IV: *Ranade*

1. Ranade eventually held the highest judicial position open to any Indian. Working in Marathi, Sanskrit, and English, he wrote and spoke on such vital subjects as re-

ligion, reform, and economics. His collection of *Essays in Religious and Social Reform* was edited by M. B. Kalaskar (see bibliog.).

2. For additional biographical material, consult G. A. Mankar, *Justice M. G. Ranade;* J. K. Kellock, *Mahadev Govind Ranade.*

3. Malabar and Coromandel were the western and eastern areas of South India.

4. This was in 1018.

5. Russian Turkestan.

6. Kutbuddin Aibak assumed the title of Sultan of Delhi after the Assassination of Muhammad of Ghur, in 1206.

7. A loin cloth.

8. Mlechchhas: Foreigners.

9. The Din Ilahi was the Emperor Akbar's attempt to establish a syncretic religion for his empire. It did not survive his death.

10. Vaishnavism, worshipping Vishnu in his various incarnations, especially those such as Krishna and Rama, is tolerant in its outlook. Even Non-Hindu personages may be looked upon as avatars, or manifestations of Vishnu.

11. The term "community" is used to refer to specific cultural groups such as Moslem, Hindu, Christian.

CHAPTER V: *Gokhale*

1. Sitaramayya, *op. cit.,* I, 89.

2. But Gokhale did refuse a knighthood. See *ibid.,* I, 64.

3. *Ibid.,* I, 90. For material on the period, consult Minto, Ranade.

4. See *Indian Nation Builders,* I, 206.

5. Chintamani, *op. cit.,* p. 61.

6. See D. S. Sarma, *Renaissance of Hinduism,* p. 141.

7. Bal Gangadhar Tilak, *Writings and Speeches,* pp. 304–305. For other biographical material consult Sastri, *Life*

of Gopal Krishna Gokhale; John S. Hoyland, *Gopal Krishna Gokhale;* M. K. Gandhi, *Gokhale—My Political Guru.*

8. European and native.

9. Lord Curzon served as Viceroy from 1899–1905.

10. Lord Ripon served 1880–1884.

11. Queen Victoria issued a proclamation November 1, 1858 which pledged Great Britain to recognize rights of Indian subjects.

12. Gokhale's speech here was delivered just two months after Japan's astonishing victory over Russia had been formalized by the Treaty of Portsmouth, 5 September 1905.

CHAPTER VI: *Tilak*

1. Lokamanya: "revered by the people." For an analysis of Tilak's ideas consult D. Mackenzie Brown, "The Philosophy of Bal Gangadhar Tilak."

2. For a commentary on the role of the Chitpawan Brahmans in Indian politics, consult Sarma, *op. cit.*

3. Speech of February, 1908. Quoted by D. P. Karmarkar, *Bal Gangadhar Tilak,* p. 165.

4. See Tahmankar, *op. cit.,* pp. 23–25.

5. See Karmarkar, *op. cit.,* pp. 43–44.

6. Actually the Nationalists felt they had virtually been excluded by the constitutional provisions forced through by the Reform wing of the party. See Sitaramayya, *op. cit.,* I, pp. 96–98.

7. The Swadeshi movement was designed to encourage the production and consumption of Indian native goods in place of British imports.

8. Quoted in Karmarkar, *op. cit.,* p. 163.

9. Dadabhai Naoroji.

10. The proclamation of 1858.

11. Chanakya was the political advisor of Chandragupta,

who conquered the ruling Nandas and established the Maurya Dynasty in India at the end of the fourth century B.C.

12. Lord Morley was Secretary of State for India, 1905–1910.

13. Sir Raghunath Purushottam Paranjpe served as a member of the India Council in London and attacked Tilak's stand on untouchability. See Tahmankar, *op. cit.,* p. 50. S. K. Damale was once the editor of one of Tilak's newspapers, the *Rashtra Mata.* See *ibid.,* p. 157.

14. *Manusaṁhitā,* VII, 27–29.

15. They were the sixth and seventh incarnations of the god Vishnu. Parashurama was defeated in combat by Rama, the hero of the epic *Rāmāyaṅa.*

16. In the later Vedic writings, Asuras are pictured as demons or enemies of the gods.

17. Tilak refers frequently to Japan, in his public speeches.

18. In 1907.

19. A bombing outrage in Bengal which British authorities contended was incited by articles in Tilak's newspaper, *Kesari.* In 1908, Tilak was sentenced to six years' hard labor.

20. Note this appeal to passive resistance by one whom the British looked upon as an advocate of extreme violence.

21. The work referred to is *Indian Unrest* by Valentine Chirol (see Bibliography).

22. The Peshwas were the hereditary ruling powers of the Maratha Confederacy after 1720. From the capital in Poona, these Brahman prime ministers controlled a large area in western India.

23. Nana Phadnavis was the leader of the Maratha ministers at Poona with whom the British negotiated the 1776 Treaty of Purandhar, after war over the possession of

the island of Salsette. Malik Amber, an African slave who rose to become prime minister of the kingdom of Ahmadnagar, led its defense against Mogul attacks during the emperor Jahangir's reign in the early 17th century. Akbar was Jahangir's father. Aurangzeb (1658–1707) was the last of the great Mogul rulers.

24. As used here, "Dharma" means duty or nature.

CHAPTER VII: *Lajpat Rai*

1. Chintamani, *op. cit.,* p. 112.

2. Among these are: *The Arya Samaj, Young India, India's Will to Freedom, England's Debt to India, The Political Future of India.* See bibliography for these titles and for his extensive series of articles published in American periodicals.

3. See Lajpat Rai's "Gandhi and Non-Coöperation."

4. For an account of his death see "Lajpat Rai Obituary, *The Nation,* 127 (November 28, 1928), p. 563. Whether or not his death was due to the beating has been disputed. See Nehru's comments on this in the quoted selection of Chapter IX.

5. The Montagu-Chelmsford *Report on Indian Constitutional Reforms* was published in 1918. E. S. Montagu was Secretary of State for India; Lord Chelmsford was Viceroy, 1916–21.

6. The Public Service Commission of 1886 issued a report which laid the foundations for later development of the Indian Public Service. It recommended the division of services into two branches: "Indian," recruited in Britain, and "Provincial," recruited in India.

7. Both Chandra Pal and Lajpat Rai had supported Tilak in the earlier struggle over the partition of Bengal.

8. Ibbetson served as Census Commissioner and as Lieutenant Governor of the Punjab.

CHAPTER VIII: *Gandhi*

1. See M. K. Gandhi, *Autobiography*, p. 185. This is the prime source for material on his life up to the time of the Champaran campaign recounted here and covers events up to 1921.

2. At its inception, the Ashram was a group of about twenty-five men and women. Some were from South Africa, others from different Indian provinces. They shared a common kitchen and common living responsibilities. See Gandhi, *op. cit.*, p. 482.

3. For a thorough analysis of these techniques, consult Bondurant, *op. cit.*, especially pp. 36–45.

4. King Janaka was traditionally the father-in-law of Rama and was king of ancient Videha in northern India. The first three sentences are taken from an early chapter in Gandhi's *Autobiography* entitled, "The Stain of Indigo."

5. The ryots were the Indian peasant laborers.

6. Kothis: companies or firms.

7. Ahimsa: non-injury.

8. Vakils: attorneys.

9. Darshana seekers: In this context the term refers to the privilege of seeing a famous or saintly person and receiving inspiration thereby.

10. C.I.D. officers were responsible for controlling criminal or treasonable activities in India.

11. Raj: rule.

CHAPTER IX: *Nehru*

1. Jawaharlal Nehru, *Toward Freedom*, p. 29.

2. *Ibid.*, p. 21.

3. See Chintamani, *op. cit.*, p. 193.

4. Nehru, *op. cit.*, pp. 39–40.

5. *Ibid.*, p. 50.

6. For his attitudes on "Communalism," see Frank

Moraes, *Jawaharlal Nehru—A Biography*, pp. 222–236.

7. *Ibid.*, p. 292.

8. From his letter from Central Prison, Allahabad, to Gandhi at Yeravada Jail, in Poona, dated 28 July 1930. Quoted in Sitaramayya, *op. cit.*, I, 640.

9. Nehru, *op. cit.*, pp. 229–230.

10. 1928.

11. The Simon Commission was appointed in 1927 to study the operations of government under the Indian Constitution. Since the Commission included members of the British Parliament only, it was boycotted in India by those who resented the failure to include a single Indian member.

12. The Mahasabha was an organization of Hindu Nationalists in opposition to Non-Hindu communal groups. See also Nehru, *op. cit.*, pp. 288, 329.

13. The Gandhian Satyagraha campaign and other struggles after the Amritsar Massacre.

14. Singh was one of two persons who threw bombs from the gallery onto the floor of the Indian Legislative Assembly.

15. Pant was a fellow inmate of Dehra Dun jail where Nehru's *Toward Freedom* was written.

CHAPTER X: *Radhakrishnan*

1. Quoted by D. B. Dhanapala, *Eminent Indians*, p. 67.

2. UNESCO carried on the program of the old League agency.

3. 1938.

4. The Government of India Act of 1935.

5. *History of Rome*, 1866.

6. The Manchurian Incident.

7. Churchill.

NOTES

CHAPTER XI: *Narayan*

1. At the University of Wisconsin he was deeply impressed by the "socialist" views of his instructors. For a brief summary of Narayan's early life, consult Yusuf Meherally's introduction to Jayaprakash Narayan's *Towards Struggle*, pp. 7–14. An exciting though inaccurate account is to be found in Dhanapala's *Eminent Indians*, pp. 144–151.

2. For his own opinion of America see Narayan, *op. cit.*, p. 54. He states there: "I spent the best part of my youth in your great country and seven of my happiest years. I went there as a student and learned much, not only from its Universities but also from its factories and farms . . ."

3. See Weiner, *Party Politics in India*, pp. 25–26.

4. Quoted by Dhanapala, *op. cit.*, p. 147.

5. Quoted in Joan V. Bondurant's "The Nonconventional Political Leader," in Richard Leonard Park and Irene Tinker's *Leadership and Political Institutions in India*, p. 293.

6. Nai Talim: New Education.

7. Bhoodan: Land Gifts.

8. Sampattidan: Money Gifts.

9. Gandhi's "march to the sea" in Western India, 1930, to make salt in defiance of the government.

10. Charkha: Spinning Wheel.

CHAPTER XII: *Bhave*

1. Sitaramayya, *op. cit.*, II, 219. Bhave is placed last after Narayan in this series. Though he is six years older, his active political career began later than Narayan's.

2. Indian Government publication, *Acharya Vinoba Bhave*, p. 23.

3. Ghandi, *op. cit.*, p. 365.

4. Quoted in *Acharya Vinoba Bhave*, p. 8. The "three-fold revolution" is "a change in people's hearts," "a change in their lives," and "change in the social structure."

5. For a readable first-hand account of Vinoba's program and activities, consult Hallam Tennyson, *India's Walking Saint*.

6. Quoted in *Acharya Vinoba Bhave*, p. 13.

7. See *Time* (Dec. 29, 1958), pp. 20–21.

8. The last part of this selection, beginning "Six months ago, I had not the least idea that God was going to make me an instrument . . ." is taken from a later speech at Sagar. Both talks were given in 1951.

9. Note how closely Bhave's views on Hindu-Moslem relations, and on communal problems in general, coincide with Ranade's outlook as expressed in the first selection in this book.

10. For the ideology behind the land gift movement consult Vinoba Bhave's *Philosophy of the Bhoodan Yajna*. See also his *Swaraj Sastra*, pp. 52–54. The Vamana incarnation of Vishnu: the God is born as a dwarf and appears before King Bali who has achieved dominion over the three worlds. The dwarf asks this king to grant him as much land as he can cover in three steps. The king agrees, and Vamana walks over the earth and heaven in two paces. He refrains from taking the third step over the infernal regions, thus leaving them in control of Bali.

11. One lakh equals 100,000. One crore equals 10,-000,000.

12. Bhave had received an invitation from Prime Minister Nehru, earlier, to come to Delhi to present his ideas to the Planning Commission.

13. Bapu: Gandhi.

14. Narada was an ancient sage described in the Rig-Veda and the Mahābhārata. He is said to have been born of Brahma, to have visited the infernal regions, and to

have written the great legal textbook, the *Code of Nārada*.

15. Daridranarayana refers to the poor or destitute.

16. Bhave has exhibited considerable contempt for American institutions and attitudes. In comparing the U.S. and Russia he comments, "On the surface it might seem that the two contestants occupying the [international] arena are the Communists led by Russia and the Capitalists under the mask of Democracy by the U.S. But ideologically the latter has lost all vitality and though it might appear doughty on the strength of its military force I do not regard it as really existent as a rival against Communism. On the other hand . . . I believe that ultimately it will be Gandhism with which Communism will have its trial of strength." K. G. Mashruwala, *Gandhi and Marx,* p. 15.

CHAPTER XIII: *Response To The West*

1. At least as a prerequisite for the effective handling of political issues.

2. Amritsar has been described above. Chauri Chaura was the scene of a later clash between Indians and police which prompted Gandhi to suspend for a time his Satyagraha program. The march to the sea to break the government's salt monopoly took place in 1930, in Gujerat.

3. Dharma: law or duty.

4. This literature, the best known example of which is Kautilya's manual of government, provided practical advice on public administration in a spirit which at times resembled the Machiavellian. For a discussion of Machiavellian realism in Indian and Western traditions consult D. Mackenzie Brown, *Indian and Western Realism.*

5. See D. Mackenzie Brown, *The Philosophy of B. G. Tilak,* p. 205.

6. Consult Giles T. Brown, "The Hindu Conspiracy."

7. See, for instance, his 1914 Poona speech, above. The

sincerity of his denial of intent to incite to violence was questioned by British officials during his court trials—resulting in his convictions. For a scholarly discussion of Tilak's motives, consult Stanley Wolpert, *Revolution and Reform in the Making of Modern India*. For a brief comparison with Gandhi's outlook, consult D. Mackenzie Brown, *Gandhi and Tilak*.

8. For an analysis of the Subhas Chandra Bose movement, consult Richard Leonard Park, *Militant Nationalism in Bengal*.

9. Kabir, Tulsidas and Ram Mohan Roy each minimized sectarian religious issues in favor of devotion and tolerance. "Bhakti" involves the worship of a personal god and stresses the concept of love.

Bibliography

The following list includes only those works which are cited in the notes and commentaries.

Banerjea, Sir Surendranath. *A Nation in the Making— Being the Reminiscences of Fifty Years of Public Life.* London: Oxford University Press, 1925. xv, 420 pp.

Bhattacharya, Berjoy Krishna. *A Short History of the Indian National Congress.* Calcutta: The Book Emporium, 1948. vii, 261 pp.

Bhave, Vinoba. *Bhoodan Yajna (Land-gifts Mission).* Ahmedabad: Navajivan, 1953. xi, 134 pp.

———. *The Principles and Philosophy of The Bhoodan Yajna.* Tanjore: Sarvodaya Prachuralaya, 1955. 36 pp.

———. *Swaraj Sastra—The Principles of a Non-Violent Political Order.* Translated by Bharatan Kumarappa. Wardha: Akhil Bharat, 1955. 95 pp.

Bondurant, Joan V. *Conquest of Violence—The Gandhian Philosophy of Conflict.* Princeton: Princeton University Press, 1958. xv, 269 pp.

Brown, D. Mackenzie. "Gandhi and Tilak," *Idea and Experiment,* III (Dec. 1953), 10–12.

———. "Indian and Western Realism," *The Indian Journal of Political Science,* XV (Dec., 1954), 265–272.

———. "The Philosophy of Bal Gangadhar Tilak—Karma vs. Jñana in the Gītā Rahasya," *The Journal of Asian Studies,* XVII (Feb., 1958), 197–206.

———. *The White Umbrella—Indian Political Thought from Manu to Gandhi.* Berkeley and Los Angeles: University of California Press, 1953. xii, 204 pp.

Brown, Giles T. "The Hindu Conspiracy, 1914–17," *Pacific Historical Review,* XVII (Aug., 1948), 299–310.

Chintamani, C. Yajneswara. *Indian Politics Since the Mutiny—Being an Account of the Development of Public Life and Political Institutions and of Prominent Political Personalities.* London: Allen & Unwin, 1940. 232 pp.

Chirol, Sir Valentine. *Indian Unrest.* London: Macmillan, 1910. xvi, 371 pp.

Dasgupta, Hemendranath. *The Indian National Congress.* Volume I. Calcutta: J. D. Gasgupta, 1946. iv, 281, vi pp.

Dhanapala, D. B. *Eminent Indians.* Bombay: Nalanda, 1947. 180 pp.

Dickson, W. P., ed. *Theodor Mommsen's History of Rome.* London: R. Bentley, 1862–1875. 4 vols.

Dubois, Abbé J. A. *Hindu Manners, Customs and Ceremonies.* Translated by Henry K. Beauchamp. 3d ed. Oxford: Clarendon Press, 1906, xxxiv, 741 pp. reprinted in 1947.

Duffett, W. E., A. R. Hicks, and G. R. Parkin, *India Today—The Background of Indian Nationalism.* New York: John Day, 1942. 173 pp.

Fisher, Margaret W., and Joan V. Bondurant. *Indian Approaches to a Socialist Society.* Indian Press Digests—Monograph Series No. 2. Berkeley: Institute of International Studies, 1956. xliii, 105 pp.

Gandhi, M. K. *An Autobiography, or The Story of My Experiments with Truth.* [Translated from the original Gujarati by Mahadev Desai]. Washington, D. C.: Public Affairs Press, 1948. xi, 640 pp.

———. *Gokhale—My Political Guru.* Ahmedabad: Navajivan, 1955. x, 67 pp.

———. *Young India 1924–1926.* New York: Viking Press, 1927. xv, 984 pp.

Gangulay, Nalin C. *Raja Ram Mohun Roy*. Calcutta: Y.M.C.A. Publishing House, 1934. vii, 229 pp.

Gokhale, G. K., *Speeches of Gopal Krishna Gokhale*. Madras: G. A. Natesan & Co., 1920. xxxi, 1029, 199, xxviii pp.

Gopal, Ram. *Lokamanya Tilak—a Biography*. Bombay: Asia Publishing House, 1956. xi, 467 pp.

Hoyland, John S. *Gopal Krishna Gokhale—His Life and Speeches*. Builders of Modern India Series. Calcutta: Y.M.C.A. Publishing House, 1947. ii, 167 pp.

Indian Government. *Acharya Vinoba Bhave*. Delhi: Delhi Publications Division, Ministry of Information, 1955. 52 pp.

—————. *The Constitution of India*. Delhi: Manager of Publications, 1949. xviii, 251 pp.

Jarrett, H. S., trans. *Ain-I-Akbari of Abu al-Fadl ibn Mubarak*. Calcutta: Asiatic Society of Bengal, 1927–1949. 3 vols.

Karandikar, S. L. *Lokamanya Bal Gangadhar Tilak—The Hercules and Prometheus of Modern India*. Poona: S. L. Karandikar, 1957. xxxiv, 655 pp.

Karmarkar, D. P. *Bal Gangadhar Tilak—A Study*. Bombay: Popular Book Depot, 1956. xix, 307 pp.

Kellock, J. K. *Mahadev Govind Ranade*. Calcutta: Association Press, 1936. ix, 204 pp.

Kinkaid, Dennis. *The Grand Rebel—An Impression of Shivaji, Founder of the Maratha Empire*. London: Collins, 1937. 329 pp.

Komroff, Manuel, ed. *Travels of Marco Polo*. New York: Modern Library, 1926. xxxi, 351 pp.

Kripalani, J. B. *Gandhi the Statesman*. Delhi: Ranjit, 1951. v, 111 pp.

Lajpat Rai. *The Arya Samaj—An Account of its Origin, Doctrines, and Activities, with a Biographical Sketch of the Founder*. London: Longmans, Green, 1915. xxvi, 305 pp.

————. "Arya Samaj, Its Aims and Teachings," *Contemporary Review*, XCVII (May, 1910), 608–620.

————. "Asia After the War," *Outlook*, CXVI (Aug. 22, 1917), 612–613.

————. "Asiatic View of the Japanese Question," *Outlook*, CXIV (Oct. 18, 1916), 384–388.

————. "Dilemma of Asia," *Independent*, LXXXVIII (Oct. 2, 1916), 16–17.

————. *England's Debt to India—A Historical Narrative of Britain's Fiscal Policy in India.* New York: Huebsch, 1917. xxiv, 364 pp.

————. "Europeanization and the Ancient Culture of India," *Annals of the American Academy*, CXLV (Sept., 1929), 188–195.

————. "Gandhi and Non-Coöperation," *Nation*, CXIII (Dec. 21, 1921), 722–724.

————. "Hindu Undersecretary for India," *Nation*, CVIII (Feb. 1, 1919), 163–164.

————. *India's Will to Freedom.* Madras: Ganesh & Co., 1921. 185 pp.

————. "International Importance of India," *Nation*, CVI (Mar. 14, 1918), 286–287.

————. "New Anglo-Persian Treaty," *New Republic*, XX (Sept. 3, 1919), 152–153.

————. *The Political Future of India.* New York: B. W. Huebsch, 1919. xxviii, 237 pp.

————. "Tagore's Philosophy," *Nation*, CIV (Jan. 4, 1917), 14–15.

————. *Unhappy India.* Calcutta: Banna Publishing Co., 1928. lxx, 565 pp.

————. "What About Asia?" *New Republic*, XVIII (Apr. 26, 1919), 421–422.

————. *Young India—An Interpretation and a History of the Nationalist Movement from Within.* New York: B. W. Huebsch, 1916. xix, 257 pp.

"Lajpat Rai Obituary," *Nation*, cxxvii (Nov. 28, 1928), 563.

Mankar, G. A. *A Sketch of the Life and Works of the Late Mr. Justice M. G. Ranade*. Bombay: Caxton Printing Works, 1902. xiii, 314 pp.

Masani, M. R. *The Communist Party of India—A Short History*. London: Derek Verschoyle, 1954. 302 pp.

Masani, R. P. *Dadabhai Naoroji—The Grand Old Man of India*. London: Allen and Unwin, 1939. 567 pp.

Mashruwala, K. G. *Gandhi and Marx* (with an introduction by Vinoba Bhave). Ahmedabad: Navajivan, 1951. vii, 117 pp.

Minto, Mary Caroline (Countess). *India Minto and Morley 1905–1910 compiled from the correspondence between the Viceroy and the Secretary of State*. London: Macmillan and Co., 1934. xi, 447 pp.

Moraes, Frank. *Jawaharlal Nehru—A Biography*. New York: Macmillan, 1956. 511 pp.

Moreland, W. H., and A. C. Chatterjee. *A Short History of India*. London: Longmans, Green, 1945. xi, 552 pp.

Naoroji, Dadabhai. *Poverty and Un-British Rule in India*. London: Swan Sonnenschein, 1901. xiv, 675 pp.

———. *Poverty of India*. London: Day, 1878. 83 pp.

[Narayan, Jayaprakash] Narain, Jaiprakash. *A Picture of Sarvodaya Social Order*. Tanjore: Sarvodaya Prachuralaya, 1955. 50 pp.

Narayan, Jayaprakash. *Jeevandan*. Bombay: Janata, [n. d.]. 12 pp. (Included in *A Picture of Sarvodaya Social Order*.)

Narayan, Jaya Prakash. *Towards Struggle—Selected Manifestos, Speeches and Writings*. Bombay: Padma Publications, 1946. 244 pp.

Nehru, Jawaharlal. *Toward Freedom—The Autobiography of Jawaharlal Nehru*, New York: John Day, 1941. xvii, 445 pp.

Orr, W. G. *A Sixteenth Century Indian Mystic.* London: Lutterworth Press, 1947. 238 pp.

Overstreet, Gene D., and Marshall Windmiller, *Communism in India.* Berkeley and Los Angeles: University of California Press, 1959. xiv, 603 pp.

Pal, Bipin Chandra. *Memories of My Life and Times.* Calcutta: Modern Book Agency, 1932. xi, 465 pp.

———. *Nationality and Empire.* Calcutta: Simba Thacker Spink Co., 1916. xxxiii, 416 pp.

———. *Swaraj—What Is It? and How to Attain It?* Bombay: Vadhwani & Co., 1922. 42 pp.

Park, Richard Leonard. "The Rise of Militant Nationalism in Bengal—A Regional Study of Nationalism." Unpublished Ph.D. thesis, Harvard University, 1950 (microfilm).

Park, Richard L., and Irene Tinker, eds. *Leadership and Political Institutions in India.* Princeton: Princeton University Press, 1959. x, 486 pp.

Radhakrishnan, Sarvepalli. *Eastern Religions and Western Thought.* Oxford: Clarendon Press, 1939. xiii, 394 pp.

———. *Education, Politics, and War.* Poona: International Book Service, 1944. 208 pp.

———. *The Hindu View of Life.* (Upton Lectures Delivered at Manchester College, Oxford, 1926). London: Allen and Unwin, 1927. 133 pp.

———. *Indian Philosophy.* London: Allen and Unwin, 1927. 2 vols.

———. *Kalki or the Future of Civilization.* Bombay: Hind Kitabs, 1948. 72 pp.

———, ed. *History of Philosophy Eastern and Western.* London: Allen and Unwin, 1952–1953. 2 vols.

Ranade, Mahadev Govind. *Essays on Indian Economics.* Bombay: Thacker and Co., 1899. iii, 328 pp.

———. *Religious and Social Reform, A Collection of*

Essays and Speeches by M. G. R., M. B. Kalaskar, ed. Bombay: Thacker and Co., 1902. vii, 289 pp.

Ranade, M. G., *et al. The Indian Nation Builders*. Madras: Ganesh and Co. [*n. d.*]. 3 vols.

Roy, M. N., and K. K. Sinha. *Royism Explained*. Edited by D. Goonawardhana and D. Das Gupta. Calcutta: Saraswaty Press, 1938. 65 pp.

Sarma, D. S. *The Renaissance of Hinduism*. Benares: Benares Hindu University, 1944. ix, 686 pp.

Sastri, V. S. Srinivasa. *Life of Gopal Krishna Gokhale*. Bangalore: Bangalore Press, 1937. 138 pp.

Sitaramayya, Pattabhi. *The History of the Indian National Congress 2d ed.* Volume 1: 1885–1935. Introduction by Rajendra Prasad. Volume 2: 1935—1947, Bombay: Padma Publications, 2 vols.: I, 2d ed., publ. 1946; II, publ. 1947.

Spear, Percival. *India, Pakistan, and the West*. London: Oxford University Press, 1949. 232 pp.

Tagore, Rabindranath. *Nationalism*. New York: Macmillan, 1917. 159 pp.

Tahmankar, D. V. *Lokamanya Tilak—Father of Indian Unrest and Maker of Modern India*. London: Murray, 1956. xii, 340 pp.

Tandon, P. D., ed. *Vinoba Bhave—The Man and His Mission*. Bombay: Vora & Co., [n. d.]. 107 pp.

Tennyson, Hallam. *India's Walking Saint—The Story of Vinoba Bhave*. New York: Doubleday, 1955. 224 pp.

Tikekar, S. R., *Gandhigrams*. Bombay: Hind Kitabs, 1947. 92 pp.

Tilak, Bal Gangadhar. *Bal Gangadhar Tilak—His Writings and Speeches*. Madras: Ganesh & Co., 1919. xi, 411 pp.

"Vinoba Bhave," *Time*, LXXIII (Dec. 29, 1958), 20–21.

Vivekananda. *The Complete Works of Swami Vivekananda*. 8th ed. Almora: Advaita Ashrama, 1950. 7 vols. (vol. VIII published in 1951.)

BIBLIOGRAPHY

Weiner, Myron. *Party Politics in India—The Development of a Multi-Party System*. Princeton: Princeton University Press, 1957. xiii, 319 pp.

Wolpert, Stanley. *Revolution and Reform in the Making of Modern India*. (Forthcoming from the University of California Press, Berkeley and Los Angeles.)

Index

Page numbers in boldface type give meanings of Indian terms as used in text.